Christopher Lloyd's
Gardening Year
Journal

Christopher Lloyd's
Gardening Year
Journal

Introduced by Fergus Garrett
Photographs by Jonathan Buckley

F

FRANCES LINCOLN LIMITED

Frances Lincoln Limited
74–77 White Lion Street
London N1 9PF
www.franceslincoln.com

Christopher Lloyd's Gardening Year Journal
Copyright © Frances Lincoln Limited 2015
Text copyright © Christopher Lloyd 2015
Photographs copyright © Jonathan Buckley 2015
except for the lily beetle, page 59 © Shutterstock/
Ian Grainger and hessian background throughout
© Shutterstock/binik

First Frances Lincoln edition 2015

A catalogue record for this book is available from
the British Library.

ISBN 978-0-7112-3682-0

Printed and bound in China

1 2 3 4 5 6 7 8 9

Contents

Introduction

Nestling into a gentle, south-facing slope in the East Sussex countryside, in the sleepy village of Northiam, is Great Dixter, a celebrated garden whose world-renowned creator has had a considerable impact on contemporary gardening.

Christopher Lloyd was born at Great Dixter in 1921, the youngest of six, and spent most of his life there. Over the leaning porch of the house, which greets you as you walk down the long, uneven Yorkstone path, was his bedroom for some thirty-four years. It was detached on three sides and provided the perfect vantage point for the great man because it jutted out like a ship's bridge. Christo (as he was known to his friends) moved into this room, which had previously been occupied by his mother Daisy, the day after she died in 1972. Today, the room remains as he left it – the only part of Great Dixter that has been allowed to gather dust.

Throughout his life Christo never lost his zest for gardening or plants, and in time he was recognised as one of the world's great gardeners. He had more than just a stamp collector's attitude to plants. Being interested in all aspects of his profession, he appreciated creativity and whimsical ideas and how he could celebrate plants through his use of them. During his many years at Great Dixter, Christo learnt to be acutely aware of the practical challenges

of running a garden, of juggling time and money, of constantly assessing and being reactive to the seasons. All this experience, coupled with his acutely observant eye and a good understanding of the science behind the art of gardening, well equipped Christo to be the legendary gardener that he became. By drawing on his inquisitive mind and masterful command of the English language, Christo wrote expressively on a whole range of gardening issues – his mind always brimming with ideas. Sometimes he described people, sometimes birds, bees or bugs, at other times he covered art and music, and occasionally he wrote about food, yet in almost every case there was a link back to Great Dixter – the place that he knew and understood so well. With his willingness to teach and pass on information, Christo influenced many (including me) through his words and his creativity.

The 2.5-hectare/6-acre site of Great Dixter is shallowly terraced, takes in the terrain on all sides and wraps around a grandiose, fifteenth-century medieval house restored, renovated and added to by the great British architect Sir Edwin Lutyens. The garden is divided and subdivided into a series of rooms by balustrade yew hedging, old farm buildings and brick walls coped in Kentish tiles. The countryside floods in with long meadow grass jostling with the borders, with everything softened by vegetation, self-sowers in the walls dripping out of the crumbling lime mortar, climbers wrapping themselves around buildings and plants spilling on to the pathways. All of this provides the most intimate feel imaginable. The buildings are a testament to Lutyens's empathy with local materials – the old and new beautifully married. The gentle lines are easy on the eye and the landscape. Great Dixter's complex roofs, in layers of soft terracotta with softly swept eaves connecting one angle to another, fall low and sweep to the ground. Although the majestic house is low hung, it rises above the surroundings like an imposing ancient bastion as the land drops away on its southern flank.

I would see Christo walk the long border several times in a single day, notebook in hand, stopping in the same spot over and over again. Since his death in 2006,

the garden at Great Dixter has remained unmistakably the place that he so loved and its significance is still relevant in the horticultural world – as a place of inspiration where trends are made and not followed. Some of the old combinations have gone, and parts of the garden may have a different feel, yet the stock beds in the high garden are more intensive and vibrant than ever. The exotic garden has less of an emphasis on cannas and dahlias and instead has a heavier bias towards large leaves. Its jungle-like atmosphere is lush and green, with a canopy of bananas (*Musa*) and large rice-paper plants (*Tetrapanax papyrifer*). The solar garden continues to be bedded out in colourful ephemerals, and true to the Dixter style none of these seasonal combinations is repeated – even if they may have set the garden alight. Most of the new plantings are experimental – Dixter never rests on its

laurels (spotted laurels, as Christo would say) and of course the road to success is littered with failures. After all these years, our systems and actions remain the same. Everything is assessed and analysed, edited and fine-tuned, or swept away if need be. Changes are not made just for change's sake, but because they are improvements – with every ingredient under close scrutiny.

Christo's style remains relevant today because his garden has a certain domestic intimacy that people connect with – each of Great Dixter's many compartments or little vignettes can be related to. The planting is mixed and some of the borders are wide and deep, but this could all be scaled down to suit the needs of any gardener. Yet the most important attraction of Great Dixter for many visitors is the energy and zest behind each association, the willingness to embrace colour, the freedom to experiment and be inquisitive, the readiness to take risks and make mistakes, to welcome self-sowers, to use annuals and half-hardy perennials, to allow climbers to romp into trees and shrubs, and to plant in layers so that snowdrops, crocuses and miniature daffodils among others can sit in between hostas. Christo's way was flexible – his attitude always positive – and gardeners can take a leaf out of his book by being as intensive as they wish or practise his horticultural ideas with restraint.

Above all, Great Dixter encourages visitors to garden with freedom using the plants that they like, that grow well and work for them, in a way that pleases them. They need never worry about being judged or people looking over their shoulder while they garden creatively for the right reasons – for self-satisfaction and delight.

Fergus Garrett, April 2015

January

Dixter is rich in topiary and that always looks extra-comical when the dark figures, especially the 'peacocks', are snow-capped. Caps of snow also suit the sere remains of perennials that we deliberately refrain from cutting down in autumn: lofty cardoons are the most prominent, but there are also sedums and yarrows. All the dark evergreens come into their own, by way of contrast to the dazzling white, and not least among these are the self-sown ivies clambering up our more or less threadbare deciduous trees, in particular the ashes. Ash trees' branches are thick right to the black bud tips of their smallest twigs. The wind soughs in them to a hollow tune, but they are never dense. Much light filters through, even at midsummer, so they are the wild ivies' favourite hosts.

Ever green

Evergreens in the high garden

Gardening literature will always emphasize the importance of evergreens, in a garden, as something to look at in the winter. True, but there are evergreens and evergreens. Some of them look pretty battered or threadbare by January – *Eucryphia × nymansensis* 'Nymansay', for instance. It is a reluctant evergreen anyway, losing half its leaves in autumn.

In the high garden, straight paths form a cross and there is a square, paved area which provides a resting point (while you decide which way to turn) where they meet. I have made this a fairly important centrepiece with a preponderance of evergreens. I (unofficially) call it conifer corner.

A feature in this square is a large, thick-pencil-shaped *Chamaecyparis lawsoniana* 'Ellwood's Gold' – only noticeably golden on its young shoots in spring. Then the two 1.8m/6ft cones, now growing into each other but still individuals, are of *C. thyoides* 'Ericoides'. The softness of these and many other selected conifers is on account of all their foliage being of the juvenile type, retained in these cases right through their lives. It gives them an attractive featheriness. The normal summer colouring is sea-green, but this changes to rich purple in autumn. By now, however (and, I always feel, prematurely, but nothing can reverse

the reaction), the colour has changed most of the way back to green.

In front of the pair of chamaecyparis is a planting of the inestimable *Helichrysum splendidum*, which is one of the few ever-grey shrubs that does not look depressed beneath grey winter's skies. Its stiffly upright shoots terminate in a loose rosette of small leaves. The success or failure of this little shrub (I never let it exceed a height of 60cm/2ft) depends entirely on its being regularly hard-pruned back each spring. The result looks crude at the time but comeliness is soon restored and no flowering occurs. The mingy little yellow flower heads could attract nobody. And a no-pruning treatment results in a scraggy shrub.

Next to this group is the contrasting *Thuja occidentalis* 'Rheingold', which is a 1.8m/6ft cone of burnished golden yellow in winter. This is its best season, but it never

lets you down. I have a dark background for it in the almost too widely planted *Prunus laurocerasus* 'Otto Luyken'. This is a compact cherry laurel of rather upright habit, with rich green, highly glossy and sharply pointed oval leaves. In a border setting, its growth needs to be controlled from time to time, but not so frequently as to make it look a characterless dumpling. A hard cut-back once in seven years or so will do the trick. The white flowers are borne on loose spikes, both in spring and again in autumn, after which you can give just an annual tidying, by removing the flowered shoots.

Nearby is a silver fir, *Abies koreana* – my second of this species, because I am liable to grow a tree where there is no space for it in maturity. I enjoy it as a juvenile and then cast it out, wasting no sentiment over the loss. The reason for this fir's being so popular is that its dwarf form cones, or is expected to cone,

Skeletons of ornamental grasses play a large role in the winter garden, especially the various cultivars of *Miscanthus sinensis*. *Miscanthus sinensis* 'Silver Feather' features here in the high garden.

as quite a baby. The cones are tubby upright candles borne on the upper side of horizontal lateral branches and on quite minuscule specimens. They vary in colour, sometimes dove-mauve, sometimes (if you are lucky) navy-blue. All *A. koreana* are seedlings, so there is a good deal of variation. You might easily purchase a seedling of the vigorous type, which is just what happened to me. My tree has shot up and coned very little.

I do not like January any more than the next man,
but at least the evenings are getting noticeably longer.
By the end of the month, we have won almost an
hour of daylight in the afternoons.

....
....
....
....
....
....
....
....
....
....
....
....
....
....
....
....
....
....
....
....
....

Flowering shrubs

It has often been written that the earliest-flowering rhododendrons of the new year – *Rhododendron mucronulatum* and the even earlier *R. dauricum* – look admirable in the company of *Hamamelis mollis*, their flowers being a contrasting mauve or purple. So I dutifully planted *Rhododendron dauricum* 'Mid-winter' next to one of my old witch hazels, and it is true. They do coincide, but the rhododendron is so tempting to pick and its flowers are anyway so frost tender, that I don't give it much of a chance to make a decent bulk.

The lily-of-the-valley-scented *Mahonia japonica* started flowering in November and continues into March, but reaches a peak now with its clustered strands of small, pale yellow bell flowers. You can bring its branches into the house for a day but it is not really much use when cut and pilgrimages should be made to it, in the garden.

The shrub honeysuckle, *Lonicera* × *purpusii*, really comes into its own, now, having opened a few desultory flowers since late autumn. It is possibly at its best in the garden in February, but if picked in January it makes a great display indoors.

The fragrance from sarcococcas is by no means refined but welcome, especially at this season. Their tiny white flowers are strung along young shoots. *Sarcococca hookeriana*, its pink-tinged variety *digyna*

Winter-ripening *Aucuba japonica* f. *longifolia*, a female, is smothered in large red berries, in some years, and as they have only just fully ripened they are singularly fresh. Beside it is winter-flowering *Mahonia japonica*, which is not a very striking shrub but has fragrant, lemon-yellow flowers over a long season.

and the rather lower-growing var. *humilis* (45cm/1½ft) all have a suckering habit, good for ground-covering or infilling purposes. I have never seen fruit on them but *S. confusa* is free with its black berries, ripe from the previous year when the next year's flowers are out. *Sarcococca ruscifolia*, at 1.2m/4ft, is rather taller than the others and makes the handsomest shrub. Its berries are dark red. With all these, I prune occasionally and when the mood takes me, by thinning out old branches.

The evergreen *Clematis cirrhosa* var. *balearica* is flowering away merrily, with its palest green bells, freckled with tiny dots within, if you look for them. The larger, bolder-flowered cultivar 'Freckles' is heavily marked brownish red within and this is the more readily seen because the flowers open out quite wide. It has a long season. Unfortunately, the foliage is coarse.

Evergreen perennials

This is where I should wax lyrical on winter colour in bergenia foliage, their beautiful shades of beetroot and red and the proud carriage and outlines of the best varieties. Alas, they hate me. I don't mean that I cannot grow them – it would be almost impossible to kill one – but that their sombre, slug-hole-riddled, leather leaves are very far from making a joyful winter contribution. The only one that achieves a hint of self-respect is *Bergenia purpurascens*. I like its cheeky, prick-eared habit and its abundant May flowering on good long stems.

Phormiums border on tenderness but *Phormium cookianum* subsp. *hookeri* 'Tricolor' is flatteringly foolproof. Its arching leaves have narrow purple margins and are striped alternately in green and cream, at different widths, within. It looks as great at winter's end as at the start and will become quite exciting in early summer when it puts up flowering stems, which it regularly does. It then rises from 1m/3ft to nearly 2m/7ft.

My other phormium is the 1.5m/5ft 'Sundowner', in which bands of pink are the notable feature, along with cream and green, the margins purple, again. That is far less hardy, but may survive a mild winter without any damage. In spring, it'll want tidying up. When phormiums become large and thick and difficult to keep looking pristine, they really need replanting, but this

With a touch of sunlight on it butcher's broom certainly transforms a winter's day.

is a mammoth task. I don't blame anyone for shirking it. Furthermore, they always sulk for a year, even following a spring disturbance, which is the safest.

Some evergreen ferns remain great allies through the dark months, notably the rather lacy-leaved form of *Polypodium interjectum* called 'Cornubiense'. Only 23cm/9in or so tall, its slowly creeping habit becomes a mat and its vivid green colouring is especially welcome just now. I have moved some of this alongside my hermaphrodite form of butcher's broom, *Ruscus aculeatus*, which is covered all winter (some years better than others) with large, bright red berries, these set off by the gloomiest green foliage conceivable.

Hart's tongue ferns, *Asplenium scolopendrium*, are a standby now. They self-sow in particular in the cracks and along the foot of brick walls cemented with lime-

rich mortar. The ferns make bouquets of strap leaves and they show up well now that deciduous plants and shrubs around them have virtually disappeared. Another good'un is *Polystichum setiferum* 'Pulcherrimum Bevis' – a large clump-maker with elegant bipinnate fronds that draw to a fishtail point. That is a feature for most of the year and associates handsomely with contrasting foliage like ivies, fatsia, fatshedera and, in

summer, *Clerodendrum bungei*, all of them shade-tolerant, so there will be plenty of nourishment and moisture available.

I must also squeeze in a mention of the rusty-back fern, *Asplenium ceterach*, introduced by my mother to one of our stone retaining walls. It is an inspiring little plant, with crenately lobed foliage, rusty on the back. It very gradually spreads by running along the cracks.

Bulbs

Flowering without protection from the new year is the very short-stemmed, little *Iris histrioides* 'Major'. This is pale blue and very charming. These small bulbs are really most easily appreciated when quite thickly planted in large clay pans. Some I bring into the great hall (which is suitably chilly) as they are opening; some stand on a chest in the porch and others on the paving just outside the porch. After they have finished their growth cycle, we repot for the next season, but first roll the dormant bulbs in a fungicidal powder to protect them against inkspot which is a killer.

'Katharine Hodgkin', though classified as a reticulata hybrid, is definitely similar to *I. histrioides* in habit but far more robust. The flowers are rather sinisterly marked in shades of grey, pale blue and yellow, all of them fairly subdued, but they make a great

Above: *Galanthus* 'Atkinsii' is a strong, rather tall-growing hybrid that clumps up amazingly fast and makes an excellent infill in a border of summer perennials.

Left: *Iris reticulata* takes its turn with summer-flowering *Geranium* 'Mavis Simpson'.

display. 'George' is rather taller, and more obviously has *I. reticulata* in its blood, but is still early. This is purple and scented. *Iris winogradowii* is very close in appearance to *I. histrioides* 'Major', but soft, pale yellow.

Iris unguicularis is not bulbous, but comes in apropos as a generally winter-flowering species. The commonest colour is mauve, its large, fragile blooms (large for the time of year) of silken texture. Its buds are lovely to pick for the house the day before they would open anyway. They may be borne at any time from late October to the end of March, this depending on the variety and on the weather. In every mild spell, you should visit them on alternate days, to gather the next crop. The plants are extremely untidy and should be sited in a hot position, handy for picking but not prominently in sight. The advantage in leaving the old foliage is that this encourages the flower buds to make longer stalks for picking.

In normal seasons, most snowdrops belong to February, but it is a big group and there are exceptions. Chief among them at Dixter is *Galanthus* 'Atkinsii'. This makes a great show in a damp, north-west-facing border which is primarily given over to *Euphorbia palustris*, *Aralia cachemirica*, *Rodgersia pinnata* cultivars and *Geranium wallichianum* 'Buxton's Variety'.

Bay laurel

The most important evergreen at Great Dixter is the bay laurel, *Laurus nobilis,* alongside the front path as you approach the house on foot. I don't know its age. It was there before 1910 and you cannot cut it down and count the rings as it is, basically, a multi-stemmed shrub, though of tree-like proportions and some 6m/20ft high. Bay green is descriptive of a colour – a singularly warm shade without any hint of blue, but, rather, of yellow. This is emphasized in winter sunlight.

Its branches are highly flexible and get weighed to the ground if there is a heavy fall of snow. But they bounce back. Prolonged, hard frost can be a problem. At the end of a really hard winter, the tree will turn brown and look dead. The temptation is to cut it right down, and to wait for regrowth from the base. Don't be in a hurry, but do make a start, in the spring, by cutting branches cleanly back to quite thick wood. Then wait, patiently, and by early July (no sooner) you will see tiny sprouts of young growth buds appearing out of the old wood.

The bay tree flowers, briefly but beautifully, most years in early May – an abundance of pale yellow blossom lining the young shoots, and wafting an etherealized bay fragrance if the air is warm and damp. In our case, almost the entire display is created by stamens, as we have a male tree.

When branches snap off our bay tree they are joyfully put on my fire. The smell from bay-leaf smoke is intense and satisfying. The leaves being large, the blisters that form on them as they heat are large and resound, as they burst, in a loud cannonade.

Other jobs for the month

Clearing snow

O Unless the paths are quickly cleared, snow soon packs down and freezes, becoming slithery.

O Beat branches with a stick, while the snow is falling, even in a blizzard, even in the night, to prevent the weight of snow from accumulating.

Self-sowns

O Keep weeding. The appearance of certain annual weed seedlings, in January, is always a signal that the year has turned. Notable are the redoubtable goose grass or cleavers – we're always at that – and ivy-leaved speedwell, *Veronica hederacea*, which is not too serious a weed and belongs only to the first half of each year, but can utterly wreck the appearance of carefully prepared spring bedding, so we have to take it seriously.

Dealing with the produce

O Barring accidents, there should be a plentiful supply of vegetables from the garden, so crop it regularly.

O Use leeks, carrots, salsify, parsnips, celeriac and Jerusalem artichokes straight from the ground. That gives the best flavour.

O As celeriac is not very frost-hardy, cover the plants with hessian during frosty spells.

O Take 'Pink Fir Apple' potatoes and shallots out of storage.

O Pick saladings such as rocket, chervil, pak choi, mizuna, mega-cress, lamb's lettuce and winter radish.

O Harvest sprouts (two kinds, early- and late-maturing), the savoy cabbage 'January King', which I find has the best flavour, and the first of the purple-sprouting broccoli.

February

I like February: I like the word and I like the feeling of so much, in my garden, being on the move. A recent entry in my small pocket diary for 13 February tells me that tortoise shell butterflies were feeding on crocuses and snowdrops and that there was a peacock butterfly on *Coronilla valentina*. Definitely elevating to the spirits. Another good sign is that the great crested newts are back in the ponds. From now on, they abound particularly in the sunk garden pool, where they are a great source of interest to visitors from April on. The water there remains pretty clear for most of the year and you can also admire the purplish underwater rosettes of *Stratiotes aloides*, the water soldier.

The best of Dixter in February

The flowers

On average, most snowdrops are at their peak this month. I love to pick a fat bunch and to have them near me indoors where I can inhale their honey scent. Bees go to them for their nectar. Snowdrops thrive especially where there is a bit of shade and the turf (if they are in a meadow setting) is a little less dense than out in the open. A few snowdrops among the foliage of *Cyclamen hederifolium* look nice.

Early narcissus are tremendously welcome. One that does well with me but that you seldom see in gardens is *Narcissus tazetta*, the species itself, parent of a large proportion of the bunch-headed kinds with the strongest (not the pleasantest) scent. It has a wide southern European distribution in the wild. Because it is on the tender side, I grow it under a warm wall. It has a very long-flowering season and was already under way last month. The leaves are dark green, contrasting with white flowers (the cup, cream) in a large cluster which open in succession.

'Tête-à-Tête' is deservedly popular. We are told that all stock of it is infected with virus disease, but it has tremendous vigour none the less. A small yellow trumpet, rather lacking in class, if I may say so, about 23cm/9in tall and tremendously willing. It looks nice with the pale yellow of primroses.

Narcissus minor is a dear little yellow trumpet, 15cm/6in tall, with twisted leaves. It clumps up well, even in rough meadow conditions. As it is about half the size of, though otherwise similar to, our native Lent lily, *N. pseudonarcissus*, I like to keep the two of them separate. We have a lot of the latter in front of the house, where it self-sows. It may not be at its best till March, but is nearly always finished by even an early Easter.

In a really cold winter, the tallish yellow *N. cyclamineus* hybrid 'February Gold' would not start flowering till March, but in other years it lives up to its name. I have it in a rather pleasing planting at the bottom of the long border, where it rubs cheeks with the margins of my main planting of Lenten roses, generally known as *Helleborus orientalis* hybrids. These look clean and pristine, because we remove their tired old leaves well before the display gets going. These hellebores are in mixed shades, mostly light colours, which show up better than the dark.

The subshrubby *H. argutifolius* has great bouquets, almost like a mop-headed hydrangea, of pale green flowers above handsome trifoliate leaves with mock prickles along their margins. It never lasts for long with me. Neither does *H. foetidus*, our native stinking hellebore, which I really prefer. After flowering, it is apt to go to pieces,

Right: *Narcissus* 'Tête-à-Tête' stand out among the foliage of *Geranium malviflorum* and verbascum.

Below: Snowdrops and *Cyclamen hederifolium* provide winter interest amongst dormant fern crowns.

but there will be others. It makes rich, dark evergreen leaves with narrow segments, above which the pale green inflorescence is well framed. The bell flowers are rimmed in purple. This hellebore often places itself at the foot of deciduous shrubs. It is shade-tolerant but comes truly into its own in winter, when the shrub is naked.

Helleborus × *nigercors* is a particularly handsome hybrid between the Christmas rose, *H. niger*, and *H. argutifolius*, which used to be called *H. corsicus* – which explains the ugly hybrid name. This seems to be pretty long-lived with me and has bold leaves and long-flowering trusses of large white blooms. In the last part of its flowering, it will contrast well with a neighbouring clump of the cyclamineus hybrid daffodil 'Jetfire', which is yellow with a short, pale orange trumpet.

On the lower terrace grows *Daphne odora* f. *alba* 'Aureomarginata', and that will flower from now till well into April, generously scenting the air with a heavy fragrance. The flowers are borne in terminal clusters on the young shoots and are purplish pink on the outside, almost white within. The evergreen leaves are rather ugly, the more so as the situation is too hot and sunny (but nicely sheltered from cold winds), and this turns it a rather sickly green. Like *D. mezereum*, this is excellent on limy soils.

I don't mind *Helleborus foetidus*, here at the foot of *Cotoneaster horizontalis*, being short-lived as it self-sows and is already looking its handsomest in its second year.

Winter crocuses

February is the month of winter crocuses – *Crocus tommasinianus*, *C. flavus* subsp. *flavus*, *C. sieberi* and *C. chrysanthus* with its innumerable variants. All of them adapt well to life in meadow turf and most self-sow.

Crocus flavus subsp. *flavus* is small but an intense and vital shade of pure, rich orange. It is fertile and self-sows.

Crocus chrysanthus, shaped like an electric light bulb when closed and bowl-shaped when open, has an incredibly wide range of colour forms. 'Advance', for instance, is pale yellow on the inside and mauve outside. My favourite is one bred by Ernest Bowles, 'Snow Bunting' (see below). Cream-white with dark striping; sometimes a rather ragged petal outline and a gorgeous honey scent. It is one of the earliest in bloom, but often, alas, a different white crocus is sold under this name.

Frost protection

The old greenhouse has solid walls, for the sake of insulation. The glass sides are half and the roof entire Dutch lights. There are benches all round, covered with grit, and the floor is earth. The great idea is to be able to retain a humid atmosphere when sun heat is strong. In this way we do not need to shade the glass at all.

Since Fergus came in 1993, two new greenhouses have gone up. One is alongside the old one and is the same size. In the original one, we aim to keep the temperature just above freezing, at its lowest. In the extension, we house our really tender, subtropical plants (see below) and here we aim (using an electric blower heater) to maintain a minimum temperature of 10°C/50°F. The third, separate, house is a pit – the lower half of which is below ground level. Plants love it in there.

'Lure' is a word we hear a lot. Plants are 'lured' into premature growth or flowering, we are told, as though there were some evil genius, out there, pulling strings and drily cackling as he (she wouldn't be capable of such a thing) watches the approach and consummation of disaster.

Pruning

Naturally, it is simpler to prune a deciduous shrub, like a rose, when it has no foliage on it and you can clearly see the whole plant's structure and what treatment will suit it best. That applies to all the deciduous flowering shrubs. You are supposed to prune a philadelphus immediately after flowering. But if you do, you will be working in conditions too congested and leafy to be able to see exactly what you are doing, and it is extremely easy to knock off brittle young shoots by accident. By leaf-fall, all growth has hardened up and it is easy to work without doing damage. As with the fig (see below), you have the latitude to do the pruning any time up to the flushing of a new crop of leaves. Meanwhile, all the wall-trained pears and the espalier Comice pears in the high garden are pruned by spurring back last year's young shoots.

Other jobs for the month

Routine care

- Weed, rejuvenate and manure hardy perennial beds. Split perennials such as aconites, crocosmias, phloxes and lilies.
- Ensure the cultivated area is clear around young trees for the first few years. Then lay on a topdressing of garden compost. This, of course, also feeds the neighbouring turf, but this can't be helped.
- Clean out all the yew hedge bottoms, as they will die out if they have to compete with a lot of weed growth around their feet. Then feed the hedge roots.
- Clean off annual weeds.
- Prune summer-fruiting raspberries, gooseberries and currants. Then apply a thick mulch of garden compost to the whole area.
- Mulch rhubarb well with compost.

Seed ordering

- Get down to the major task of deciding which seeds to order from which merchants, for the coming year. At the same time, make notes on what you would like to use and combine in different parts of the garden. That's the exciting bit.

Annual overhauls

This is an old, old story. We all know about sending the mowers into dock in winter and the circular saw in for sharpening in summer, but any piece of machinery that has been given a rest for a while, far from feeling young and invigorated, gets into a state of torpor from which it refuses to be aroused – except by the expert. By the time the mower's problem has been resolved, the weather will have changed.

March

There is something sharp and aggressive
in the very word. March is prepared to hurl
every sort of weather at us. It is the first month
of spring but winter still lurks in the wings,
ready to return with an ugly leer. Snow is
more frequent than in December. Yet it is a
jokey sort of snow. As it sits perched on top
of blue grape hyacinths and yellow daffodils,
we can scarcely take it seriously and, indeed,
it is gone within minutes, until the next
squall arrives. Winds are vicious too.

Erythroniums

My main colonies of the European dog's-tooth violet, *Erythronium dens-canis* (see below), are here and they are at their peak for ten days mid-month. First, and very suddenly, you see a dark, chocolate-coloured cluster of unfurling leaves, with narrow flower buds nestling at the centre. Within a very few days, the leaves have expanded, showing a marbled pattern of chocolate and green, while the buds have stretched upwards on 10cm/4in stalks, only waiting for a warm morning to open their nodding blooms into a kind of lampshade with rosy-mauve petals at the horizontal or, if feeling expansive, reflexed.

In a month's time, but I may as well mention it here, quite a different, albeit similarly coloured, erythronium, the American *E. revolutum*, will be flowering. It is spreading fast, with its running rootstock.

When that Aprilis, with his showers swoot,
The drought of March hath pierced to the root,
And bathed every vein in such licour,
Of which virtue engender'd is the flower;

Chaucer, The Canterbury Tales

Meadows

The meadow areas are the most colourful and interesting, this month. In its first half, the Dutch crocus hybrids, *C. vernus*, are at their peak – purple, mauve, stripy, white – and not in the least demure. They have self-sown freely over the years and there are wonderfully thick areas of them that make your heart bounce, given a sunny spring day (and they do occur).

By the front path, they coincide with the Lent lilies, *Narcissus pseudonarcissus*, which are equally generous self-seeders. In the orchard, the crocuses form a swathe, roughly parallel with the long border and wrapping round the feet of the circular steps. They overlap the daffodils, but make good team-mates, as the daffodils are still short enough not to interfere with the crocuses' display. Finally, they fill the bath-shaped basin of the drained upper moat. Originally, my mother planted them on the sloping sides, but they soon seeded all over the more moist bottom.

At one end of this dry moat is a patch of summer snowflakes, *Leucojum aestivum*, and this usually reaches its peak after the crocuses have faded, when the wild celandines, *Ficaria verna*, are flowering all over.

One of my mother's additions was *Anemone apennina*, in weakish shades of blue, pink and off-white. It is happy enough and interesting for its circle of far

Dutch hybrids of *Crocus vernus* and native Lent lilies, *Narcissus pseudonarcissus*, have self-sown in the front entrance meadow garden.

more numerous petals than our own wood anemones, *A. nemorosa*. These, although never planted deliberately, are abundant in many places, especially all around the lower moat, which is at the bottom of the orchard. These blush-white anemones (the blush becomes more intense as the flowers age) grow in carpets, but are mixed in with clumps of wild primroses, the softest shade of yellow. There are also patches of goldilocks, *Ranunculus auricomus*, a small, bowl-shaped buttercup and the earliest of its genus to flower. The anemones open wide by day and with slight encouragement from the weather. The scene is as good as anything we have deliberately contrived.

Elsewhere we have established the rather small-flowered doronicum, or leopard's bane, with yellow, spring-flowering daisies on 75cm/2½ft stems, that you see so much of in woodland in the north and into Scotland.

Alders are the poor relations of birches, in the popularity stakes, but I have a weak spot for them. They like the same moist conditions as willows.

There is one other meadow area which should be looked at now, next to the boiler room at the east end of the house. There are ancient lilacs, now in bright green bud, and then a deep hollow, once a pond but drained by my father into the lower moat. However, we also drain into it surface water from the high garden area, and there is a leaky hydrant by the raspberry cage, which is never dry for long, however much I plead for corrective action. That drains into the hollow and we have now taken advantage of the inevitable and planted it with kingcups, *Caltha*. There are also clumps, here, of a handsome red-flowered comfrey which I first collected from a ditch-side in Romania (Transylvania), some twenty years ago.

Around this hollow is a lively spring display of goldilocks, *Ranunculus auricomus* – our largest colony, by far; lady's smock, *Cardamine pratensis*, in contrasting mauve;

and wood anemones. On the bank, just below Big Dick, the big yew, is a favourite tree willow, *Salix daphnoides* 'Aglaia'. This is a male, but, for many weeks before flowering, it is covered with silver-white pussies, the young stems being deep crimson-red. It presents me with a cultural problem. If you never prune it, young growth, with its bright winter colouring, is much reduced, but if you do cut it back rather sternly, it dies. I am now on to my third or fourth specimen. I shall probably not prune it and see what happens. It looks nice all through the year.

One way and another, we have quite a number of different willows and these are a favourite host plant for the toothwort, *Lathraea clandestina*, which may also wander to pastures new.

We have a native *Alnus glutinosa* in the horse pond area, which my brother Oliver planted during the war, but the house cow (a Jersey), which we kept in those days, ate its leader so that it has two trunks. There is a hollow between these two which is filled with rainwater for most of the year. I like that (don't ask me why). But of late, a self-sown seedling has appeared right on the bank of the horse pond and that has streaked ahead. It flowers in February – a purplish colour, while the dormant leaf buds are blue.

My showiest alder in flower, however, is the Italian alder, *A. cordata*, which

I have toothwort on the willows by the horse pond and also on *Salix alba* 'Sericea', which I grow for its pale grey foliage, in the long border.

is planted by the lower moat. The male catkins on that are clustered like the fingers of your hand if you held them straight and parallel. At this stage, they point in any direction – often horizontally or upwards – but on flowering, this month, they hang like any other catkin and they are fat and prosperous-looking, not a bit skinny like a hazel's. A good bright yellow, too. The wind soon blows them off.

Toothworts

These are total parasites, without any green in the plant at all. *Lathraea clandestina*, which comes from southern Europe, has clusters of bright purple flowers – like an aniline dye but also easily mistaken for crocuses at a distance – from February to April and it can make a great display. Mine are fun, but I could wish that the show had a bit more punch in it. The plant is most easily established by transferring a lump from an established colony to near the roots of your chosen host.

My essential shrubs

There are some shrubs which I feel I must have. A bit of forsythia, for instance, so that I can bring budded branches of it into the house shortly before it flowers outside. *Kerria japonica*, again yellow-flowered, I must also have. I am growing the single 'Golden Guinea' cultivar.

One or other corylopsis seems essential to me, but I must have a scented kind. I therefore have the lemony-scented *Corylopsis glabrescens* with its dangles of pale yellow blossom that are nice to pick.

What I like about *Camellia japonica* 'Lady Vansittart' is the neatness of its leaves and the agreeable twist on them. The double flowers are generally pale pink, often pink with a few red petals, and occasionally all red. The neatly double red 'Margherita Coleoni' is rather good about a timely petal-shed. The vulgar streak in me gravitates to 'Mercury', which is large, bright red and slightly open in the centre of a loosely doubled bloom. I have that next to *Magnolia × loebneri* 'Leonard Messel'.

Of course, one must have a few magnolias and I am delighted with this one, which has quickly made a small, twiggy tree. You can admire its promise all through the winter and it flowers over quite a long period, now – a soft, clear and definite shade of pink, the flowers small but compensatingly numerous.

The chalices of *Magnolia × soulangeana* contrast with the spidery flowers of *M. stellata* behind. A good feature in magnolias is that they respond well to a hard prune, but you must feed them, too.

Magnolia stellata has been here, in the right angle of two retaining walls close to the daffodil orchard, since before I was born but has never made a large shrub, as it is not on good soil. No matter, it is large enough and I always welcome its reliable display of spidery, pale pink blossom. Some of its branches are very old and lichen-covered, but others, arising from those which I had cut back, are younger and more vigorous.

On the high wall dividing the upper and lower terraces, we have another original, *M. × soulangeana* 'Lennei', and that has a long season, starting this month. It is a large, loose-growing hybrid and, with its lax habit, takes up a lot of space if planted out in the open, so its position against a wall, where you can tie the main branches in, is ideal. This magnolia makes a great display and never fails, even if occasionally interrupted by frost.

Scillas and hyacinths

Under *Magnolia* × *soulangeana* 'Lennei' is a colony – one of several – of *Scilla bithynica*. It is a very pale blue species – rather too pale, at times – and a prolific self-seeder, so that a colony is soon built up. There is deepest shade under the magnolia in summer, but it is still leafless in March, so the scilla receives all the light it needs. I also grow it among common male ferns, *Dryopteris filix-mas,* outside our larder. The ferns are deciduous and currently dormant, their old fronds cleared away.

Another scilla we have is 'Rosea', the pink-flowered cultivar of *S. bifolia* – not so nice as the bright blue *S. bifolia* but still welcome. I've not thought of a good companion for that.

The best-known scilla, *S. siberica,* comes on gradually and may not be at its peak till the end of the month or later. This really is unadulterated and rich blue, the flowers bell-like and pendent. It grows splendidly under border conditions but does not last for many years in turf, with me. With some of my friends, it does.

Under the dogwoods at the back of our main bedding-out area, in the solar garden, is a pleasing little colony of dwarf bulbs: a late-flowering snowdrop that Beth Chatto gave me which she has named 'Finale'; a clump of yellow *Narcissus minor* (which increases rapidly in cultivated ground); and

× *Chionoscilla allenii* contrasts with the young, greeny yellow foliage of *Valeriana phu* 'Aurea', the chionoscilla clumps being among the somewhat rhizomatous valerian shoots. Later, the valerian grows up to 90cm/3ft or more and has moderately undistinguished corymbs of white flowers.

Transforming a space
In a most unpromising piece of ground where, otherwise, nothing much more than mosses will grow beneath an oak, I started a colony of the pale yellow form of hoop-petticoat daffodil, *Narcissus bulbocodium* var. *citrinus* (see above). It doesn't spread fast but does self-sow and is clearly in its element. Such a charmer.

There is something about the waxy artificiality of hyacinth flowers that I find most endearing and the scent is swooning, borne on the air.

a scilla/chionodoxa hybrid, × *Chionoscilla allenii*, a robust grower. This is the way we like to make use of spare space in spring. The bulbs will have finished flowering by the time I prune the dogwoods.

By the end of March, most of the florists' hyacinths are in flower. Whether categorized as early, mid-season or late, they all seem to flower more or less together in the garden. If you can leave your colonies undisturbed

they make up into thickly flowering groups. The flower spikes will vary a lot in size, but whether fairly large or small it doesn't matter; the mixture of all sizes is just what's needed. They can be very long-lived.

My favourite established colony is in the long border, of *Hyacinthus orientalis* 'Ostara', which is deep blue. The pale yellow 'City of Haarlem' is a good mixer, though I don't seem to keep it for very long. I have had it around a clump of *Lathyrus vernus*, which is a reddish purple, non-climbing pea, flowering now and next month, and also beneath the branches of *Spiraea japonica* 'Goldflame', which is brilliantly copper-coloured on its young shoots. Most gardeners prune this in spring, but if you do it doesn't make a good foliage display till considerably later. I prune it in July, just after flowering, which gives it time to make new growth on which to flush an abundance of early shoots next March.

Controlling hedges

We shall have got around to cutting all the rough hedges quite early in the month. If any yew or ilex hedge needs to be halved, this is also the best time to be doing it. When yew hedges are trimmed, you can never take them quite as far back as in the previous year. So, over the years, their bulk is sure to increase. If you never do anything to redress this situation, you end up with unbalanced monster hedges. I resent losing too much border space, in some situations, while, in others, neighbouring paths are so much overlapped that they can no longer be used.

This is when we halve our yews. It looks ugly and stark at first, but the wounds are soon healed. For the rare cases where they are not, we keep a few spare plants by us with which to stop gaps. Any self-sown yew seedlings spotted in the garden are potted up and grown on against an emergency.

Other jobs for the month

Sowing and planting
- Sow lettuce, parsley, celeriac and sweet peas in pots.
- Plant out autumn-sown annuals.

Pruning
- Ensure peaches have been pruned and trained before they flower, which is usually in early March. Cut out old, fruited wood and tie in young shoots, whose optimum length will be about 30cm/1ft.
- Spur-prune and tie in wall-trained pear trees.
- Strim old growth back on periwinkles and epimediums, to promote young shoots and to keep them in order.
- At least every other year but every year would be better, thin out bamboo clumps.

Routine care
- Finish clearing the borders of last year's herbaceous debris, split and replant where advisable, and fork in mushroom compost or fine, well-rotted bark, and spread on a dressing of Growmore at some 95g to the square metre (4oz to the square yard).
- Move along the flagstone paving cracks with a fine-spouted can, dribbling weedkiller.

Figs
To fruit well, as little pruning as possible should be practised on figs as they fruit from the tips of their previous year's young shoots, and a great many of these will have to be removed if the tree is to be trained into the wall. So we try to get away with doing this operation only every third year. If we leave it for too long, the branches break away from their ties, and the projecting growth is a nuisance.

April

Definitely not summer yet, but the swallows are back. House martins count as swallows for the purposes of seeing the first (which I never seem to, anyway). 12 April is cuckoo day, in Sussex (don't ask me why), but cuckoos, the loud monotony of whose persistent call we used to swear at, are now so rare that it is sometimes May before I hear my first. Still, the dawn chorus is terrific and the fact of its being so loud at Dixter is a pleasant reminder of the fact that our sort of garden provides a great many suitable habitats for nesting birds.

Daffodils

It is (or should be, unless the season is ridiculously early) the month of the daffodil. First to flower is Narcissus 'Princeps' – marketed to us as 'Princeps Maximus', to make it sound more important. It is like a glorified, tetraploid Lent lily. My mother picked most of them in tight bud, 'cooked' them in the bathroom hot cupboard, and would then send them to family friends. Next comes the mainstream 'Emperor' – a yellow trumpet and always reliable for a fortnight's display but no longer. Its last day, before fading, coincides with the cherry blossom opening on an early white-heart variety, which has made a very large tree by the lower moat. I remember that being planted in the early 1930s.

All these daffodils and narcissi were planted in large groups. Coinciding with 'Emperor' is 'Minnie Hume', a white narcissus mixed in with another, smaller white one, 'Lillie Langtry' (or it might have been 'Mrs Langtry') named after King Edward VII's favourite, who was popularly known as the Jersey lily.

A little later comes 'Barrii', this being named after the Barr family's famous bulb house. It is a yellow narcissus, the small cup being rimmed with orange. A lovely scent wafts from a big swathe of this. We are then done with the maincrop until the poet's narcissi follow much later, in May.

My mother considered that all should be deadheaded, after flowering, not by merely pulling the flowers off the still green stalks – that would have been an immoral shortcut – but by picking or pulling stem and all. We children were bribed with a penny a hundred, and everything was counted – by us. That was an accepted part of the rules. Meantime, the garden was opened for free to all parishioners on a Sunday when the daffodils were at their peak, and we were engaged to pick bunches of them to give to each group. We still open in the same way, but I'm afraid the daffodil picking has lapsed. So has the deadheading. The daffodils soon become engulfed in the rising tide of grasses and other meadow components.

I do not grow many daffodils in the borders, because their foliage becomes really unsightly there. Still, there are a few. One of the most spectacular, early on, is a white narcissus called 'Aflame', which has a large and brilliant scarlet cup. The flower nods slightly on its stalk, but I have a group in the high garden that can be seen as you walk up steps towards it. The cup bleaches very quickly, but retains its colour if picked young for indoors. Then, I have the triandrus hybrid 'Thalia', a bunch-headed pure white narcissus, whose leaves are reasonably discreet. It is a fantastically

Narcissus 'Emperor', in the foreground, has only a brief moment of glory in the daffodil orchard.

generous flowerer and for a long period. That, under a bamboo, looks nice with the blue flowers of *Brunnera macrophylla*.

Occasionally, I use a narcissus for bedding. One combination that has worked well is a carpet of the single, pure white *Arabis alpina* subsp. *caucasica* 'Schneehaube' (a seed strain), interspersed with the yellow, orange-centred cyclamineus daffodil, 'Jetfire'.

Succession planning

Narcissus 'Jetfire' and *Arabis alpina* subsp. *caucasica* 'Schneehaube' have both finished flowering mid-month, so we can follow with an early-flowering annual such as *Osteospermum hyoseroides* 'Gaiety', with bright orange daisies, maybe combined with the light blue *Asperula orientalis*. And they, again, will be followed by a third display. This, if you like seizing such opportunities, is the advantage of really early spring bedding.

Another good subject for it, while I'm on this theme, is *Bergenia stracheyi,* say with purple aubrieta. This bergenia has small, neat foliage and an abundance of deep pink flower clusters.

Precious blue in the meadow

Blue is a precious colour in a meadow, as so many of the wild flowers are yellow daisies or buttercups. Near the front path, *Camassia cusickii*, with tall racemes of light blue stars, will be in bloom by the end of April, swiftly followed by my most successful foreign import, the American *C. quamash*, my strain of which has deep blue stars on 30cm/1ft-tall stems. This clumps up well but also self-sows, the seeds not ripening till August.

The first of our local wild orchids, *Orchis mascula* (see below), is in its prime. It is a strong grower, sometimes 30cm/1ft tall, with quite long spikes of distinctly reddish purple flowers. The leaves can be heavily spotted purple. These early purples are scattered around but strongest in the upper moat. The pale blue Spanish bluebells have a stronghold, here, but they also come in pink and white in the orchard.

April tonight must pass away,
Tomorrow's sunrise brings us May,
What else it brings us – who can say?
Not you nor I.

This much is certain – April's tears
Foster the glory Summer wears,
And Love grows strong thro' doubts and fears
And cannot die.

Lines by my grandfather, Basil Field, 1834–1908

The best of Dixter in April

Stars of the border

A great feature, early in the month, are the four clipped specimens of *Osmanthus delavayi* on four corners of the barn garden. There are, I have worked out, about one-quarter million of the little tubular white flowers out at this time. Their scent is carried far on the air. They remain white for a mere week; then start noticeably changing to brown, but the scent does not abate for a long while. They are clipped over as soon as the display is past.

Rather a nice apron in front of one of the osmanthus is made by the celandine, *Ficaria verna*, which I found in a nearby shaw and named 'Brazen Hussy'. Its bright yellow flowers show up gleamingly against purple foliage. It is planted on the site of *Crocosmia* 'Lucifer', whose green spears take over as the celandine takes its bow and exits. Celandines in borders can be a menace and every year I have to eliminate plants which have found their way into some unwanted spot. I know of some gardens where they have taken over completely. They are sensitive to herbicides, but if there are other plants around, the task of elimination is not simple.

Another of these osmanthus looks good in a strong combination behind *Phormium cookianum* subsp. *hookeri* 'Tricolor' and the dwarf, heavily cut-leaved form of cardoon,

Cynara cardunculus, which I had from the Chelsea Physic Garden. In front of them grow some of the mauve-flowered, variegated-leaved honesty.

A group of the magenta-flowered evergreen azalea – *Rhododendron* Obtusum Group 'Amoenum' – makes a knock-out display near the forstal. With grass for a background, it looks just right.

By the end of the month, the borders will almost have filled in with fresh vegetation, and little soil will be showing. This is largely thanks to the running theme of forget-me-nots. They make an interrupted haze of blue through much of the garden and this will last till the end of May. They weld various good combinations, for instance with the bronze, evergreen foliage of *Libertia peregrinans* and the pale yellow young foliage of *Spiraea japonica* 'Gold Mound'. The forget-me-not haze needs to be, and is, balanced by strong

> *The* Euphorbia palustris *inflorescences sparkle. I suppose there must be a tiny crystal of nectar in the centre of each flower, and it catches the light.*

Arum excitement

Probably the most exciting flower of the month is *Arum creticum* (see above). In winter it displays its sharply angled, glossy green leaves, but now, late in April, it carries its bright yellow arum flowers, in which the spathe makes a spiral near to its tip. In the wild, I am told, it is most often a much less interesting cream colour, but the yellow form is rightly the one always seen in cultivation. Flowering may not last longer than a week, so the excitement really deserves a party in its honour. Then the plant rapidly goes to rest and is seen no more till the autumn.

foliage such as that of the cardoons, oriental poppies and delphiniums.

Other features which I think noteworthy would include the milk-and-roses form of *Lathyrus vernus* called 'Alboroseus' with the rich, reddish purple heads of *Bergenia purpurascens*. The usual purple *Lathyrus vernus* is nice with an old narcissus cyclamineus hybrid called 'Queen of Spain', which is a light lemon-yellow and not too vigorous. A group of deepest purple-brown *Fritillaria pyrenaica* rises behind the grape hyacinth *Muscari armeniacum* 'Blue Spike', which has a rather fluffed-out inflorescence.

Of euphorbias that shouldn't be taken for granted, *Euphorbia amygdaloides* var. *robbiae* grows in all sorts of places. It is somewhat unaccountable, as a disease often wipes a colony out, but it is adept at flourishing where you had not intended it. We have an ancient colony, perhaps forty years old, at

Tulipa 'Spring Green' looks good with lime-green
Smyrnium perfoliatum.

the very dry foot of a row of ash trees in the
farmyard area. Another in the risers of some
Lutyens steps. Others, again, self-sown, on
the kitchen drive wall, where they hobnob
with aubrietas and primroses. This is a
notably sunny spot, and the euphorbias are
said to like shade. But sun or shade is all the
same to them, and, when in a basking spot,
their lime-green inflorescences change to
ruby-red in July, which is totally unexpected.

Large clumps of aubrieta hang off the walls on the back drive.

The last happy place in which I would mention this spurge is beneath a stretch of yew hedging, in front of the house, where they consort brilliantly with self-sown wallflowers and bright purple honesty. This euphorbia's foliage makes dark, evergreen rosettes from which the flowering stems rise to 45cm/1½ft or so. The only attention they need (but it is often neglected) is the removal of all that has flowered and the foliage below,

Lily beetle

I feel obliged to mention one pest that turns up around this time, though sometimes earlier: the lily beetle (see above). It is bright red, rather handsome and hard-textured, so not too easily squashed. It feeds on the foliage of all your lilies and fritillaries. On sunny days, it sits on top of the foliage, often in mating pairs – and you must catch it, not getting so excited that you bungle, because as soon as the beetle sees what you are at, it drops to the ground and is totally invisible. It continues, with batches of slimy larvae, generation after generation, to ruin your lilies until August, and you really need to have someone chasing it up every day.

at summer's end. This cleans the colony in readiness for a new crop of leafy rosettes.

I grow both *E. griffithii* 'Fireglow' and my own 'Dixter'. Of the two, rather contrarily, 'Fireglow' has made the stronger colony. Both must be grown in full sun for their best colouring. 'Fireglow' is the brighter red but its green leaves are rather dull. 'Dixter' is a deeper red and the whole plant, leaf veins and stems included, is suffused with purplish red. *Euphorbia palustris* comes out at the same time and is my and Fergus's favourite. Its substantial inflorescences are lime-green and about 75cm/2½ft tall at the time of flowering, though taller later.

Rather on a par with euphorbia colouring and often mistaken for a spurge is the monocarpic umbellifer *Smyrnium perfoliatum*, a 60–90cm/2–3ft plant which can be worked into all sorts of places. I like it, for instance, with the parrot tulip 'Orange Favourite'.

A spring grouping that I enjoy has Jacob's ladder, *Polemonium* 'Lambrook Mauve', which is a low, clumpy plant, in front of pale yellow *Thermopsis villosa* (45cm/1½ft), which has loose spikes of pea flowers; magenta *Geranium macrorrhizum*, and a very strong Spanish bluebell, *Hyacinthoides hispanica* 'Chevithorn' (it is virtually sterile but makes fat clumps of large, pale blue bells).

Tulips

I will here give my concentrated attention to this favourite flower (favourite with Fergie just as much as with me) in its garden roles, although it continues through much of May, so I shall have to return to it.

Our heavy soil seems to suit tulips uncommonly well, and some of these colonies are now thirty years old. One of my favourites is the Darwin hybrid 'Red Matador', which is growing within the embrace of *Pinus mugo*. It is strong red but with that subtle pink flush on the outside which characterizes many tulips. When the bloom opens it reveals a magnificently marked and coloured centre.

I think tulips combine spectacularly with euphorbias. With *Euphorbia × martini*, which is fairly low but shrubby, with pale green, red-centred 'flowers', I have the viridiflora tulip 'Spring Green' and a third, in this party, is the green-flowered *Tellima grandiflora*, with scalloped basal leaves. With the bright yellow-green *Euphorbia epithymoides* and more of *E. × martini* behind it, I have two lily-flowered tulips, the scarlet 'Dyanito' and the orange 'Ballerina'. This is not so modest, but near by, with the sheaves of *Gladiolus tristis*, which is palest green, there is the mauve-flowered variegated honesty, *Lunaria annua* 'Variegata', and as blue a tulip as lilac knows how to be, 'Bleu Aimable'.

Tulips have many roles as bedding plants. For instance, the lily-flowered 'China Pink' above a carpet of pink pomponette daisies. I like to bed out 'Floristan Mix' carnations, treated as biennials, and their hummocks of glaucous foliage are an ideal background, in spring, for tulips, especially a rich red, black-centred one like *Tulipa eichleri*. Any biennial, or perennial treated as a biennial, will make a good partner. We like tulips with our lupins,

Opposite: Lily-flowered *Tulipa* 'Ballerina' goes particularly well with *Euphorbia* × *martinii*.

Below: *Gladiolus tristis* grows alongside tulips 'Blue Aimable' and 'China Pink', forget-me-nots and honesty, *Lunaria annua* 'Variegata', in the barn garden.

whose own young foliage makes a delightful background to any-coloured tulips. Bedded-out sweet Williams can make a terrific early summer display, but you'll want to pep them up in spring – with tulips, of course.

In cases such as the last two, the tulips will not need to be lifted until the lupins or sweet Williams have themselves completed their display, so the bulbs will have dried off and will be ready to harvest, anyway. But if they are with spring bedding, like bellis or forget-me-nots, they'll still be green. No matter. Don't imagine they need to be replanted, to finish off. Just lay them out on racks in a cool, airy shed and they will automatically withdraw their reserves from their leaves back into the bulbs.

When the foliage is quite sere, we harvest the bulbs (rubbing off any dirt) and, if we have the time then, but if not, later, we sort those bulbs which look large enough to flower the next year out from those which don't. All are hung up, safe from mice, in open-mesh bags, dangling from a horizontal pole (and appropriately labelled). The tiddlers will (sometimes not till early winter) be lined out in a reserve area and will there build up strength to be used again for display, in the year after their rest. In this way, our stocks of tulips never need to decline, but that doesn't prevent us from buying a lot more, each autumn.

Blossom

This word 'blossom' has a particular connotation – the spring blossom of cherries, plums, peaches, pears, almonds and apples, whether grown for fruit or for ornament. We do not have a lot of it, because ornamental blossom trees tend to be rather large passengers, once they have flowered. Also, there was the bullfinch problem. But some we do have, and also a certain number of flowering shrubs.

There is a large espalier pear on the solar chimney breast. 'That must be terribly old,' a lady visitor said to me. 'Well,' said I, 'how old are you, for instance?' 'I was seventy last week.' 'That's just about the pear's age,' I told her. 'Not so very ancient, is it?' She agreed. Fortunately, the pear is in good order, although it has lost a few of its horizontal branches. It is a culinary pear and excellent value as such in November, though its name label has long since vanished.

The old wild pear that was here, in front of the house, before we came to Dixter and either side of which yew hedging was planted, is quite a sight in bloom, although it was better still before we had to decapitate it, following the 1987 storm, which left it rocking. At least two species of parasitic fungi fruit at its base, each autumn, so I suppose its days are numbered.

Yet another old pear, a nineteenth-century survivor, is in the peacock garden,

Our old *Malus floribunda*, planted when we came to Dixter, is surrounded by a carpet of *Epimedium pinnatum* subsp. *colchicum*.

I am fond of pear blossom, for its sickly sweet scent; also for the distinct manner in which the flowers (which are always dead white) are borne in clusters.

and that is a beautiful shape, especially noticeable when flowering. From being vertical at its base, the trunk divides, about 1.2m/4ft up, into two horizontals, and these become vertical again, after another 90cm/3ft or so. My sister and I loved to hoist ourselves on to the horizontals, when we were children. The crop of small pears is prolific and always scab-free, but no one is tempted, more than once, to eat them.

The *Malus floribunda* has fantastically twisted trunks. Its crab blossom is best mid-month, while still not quite out, and is then a lively shade of pink, but it soon bleaches.

There used to be six 'John Downie' crabs, in front of the house, this being the best for jelly-making, though the fruit is subject to scab. Growing on particularly nasty clay, they never really throve and only one now remains – pink as the blossom opens, then fading white.

Cherry blossom

I have two of the bush cherry *Prunus glandulosa* 'Alba Plena' (see above) in the barn garden, wreathed with double white pom-poms along all the previous year's young shoots. I prune it hard, after flowering, to encourage plenty of new growth, so it is never more than 1.2m/4ft tall. Some 'Red Shine' multiple-stemmed tulips looked spectacular in front of the prunus. In autumn, the cherry's foliage turns pink. Meanwhile the morello cherry is trained against a north wall in the barn garden. That is pure white, and we have planted, alongside it, the double form of *P. cerasus* called 'Rhexii'. It makes a beautiful companion in its flowering season, but does not fruit.

Pots of colour and scent

Hyacinths look and smell wonderful when gathered together in large pots and I buy at least twenty-five of each variety at a time. They do more than one year, and are eventually planted out. Of the late kinds, one of the most successful is the old double red *Hyacinthus orientalis* 'Hollyhock' – a compact cultivar which needs no staking. 'King Codro' is an intriguing late-flowerer; deep blue but with green tips to its petals. It lurches about, rather, but is endearing, like some friends who have a weakness for the bottle, but always remain charming under the influence.

Narcissi can often be flowered in the same pot for two or three successive years. *Narcissus* 'Quail' is an excellent, multi-headed, long-flowering jonquil, deep butter yellow. 'Sir Winston Churchill' is a multi-headed tazetta – the scent is quite different from a jonquil's and not so friendly. This has an orange cup but prominent white doubling in the centre. You can choose any tulips you like for pot work. I am fond of the early, deep yellow, single *Tulipa* 'Bellona', which is also sweetly scented, but all too often I have been sold the wrong tulip under this name. A protected position will enable you to grow double tulips, especially the heavy-headed late doubles, without them being snapped off beneath the weight of rain. 'Prinses Irene' is a winner of subtle colouring.

Fergus brings out, as early as he dares, the yellow-variegated form of *Agave americana*, to give solidity to the scene. That will stick around till October. We also like to put *Geranium maderense* on display, if it is flowering, but it can be ruined by a late frost.

Other jobs for the month

Sowing

- O Sow broad bean seed and most of the peas – both in considerable quantity, as they freeze so well.
- O Make outdoor sowings of, for example, parsley, lettuce, beetroot and possibly spinach.
- O Any F1 brassicas that need sowing this month or next should be done under controlled conditions, in pots, under glass.
- O Sow leeks in pots, transferring them to their purpose-made trenches in June.
- O Sow flower seeds under cold glass. The seedlings need full light as soon as they have germinated.

Potting on

- O Prick out or pot seedlings up individually.
- O Pot on individually any rooted cuttings that were overwintered under glass.

Dealing with produce

- O Harvest purple-sprouting broccoli, kale and sprouting Brussels sprout shoots.
- O Keep cropping all the saladings that overwintered successfully.

I am always trying to impress on my seed-sowers that they should not sow too thickly, which is the temptation if plenty of seed is available.

May

Temperatures are all over the place, in May, but one of the moments that I'm strongly aware of is when, near noon, I'm beneath newly leaved trees, the sun is standing really high and the shadows are short. The sharpness of spring will be present for a long time, but the closeness to summer suddenly makes itself apparent.

The belt of ash trees on our west flank is still unyielding, in the first half of the month; no rustle of spring from them; only the empty sough of winter. Yet even they have to relent and put on their summer apparel, by the end of the month. Their character is utterly transformed. Also, the young oak foliage is fresh as fresh, in May. By the forstal, the oak trees make a fine, though suitably distant backdrop to the horse pond.

In the meadows

There is a great surge of growth in the meadow areas, one of whose most exciting features is the huge quantity of green-winged orchids, *Anacamptis morio*, which have naturalized since my mother and I introduced them from the wild in the 1930s. Their natural habitat was permanent pasture, but when all of that disappeared during the war, because there were ploughing grants, the orchis went too. So what would now be considered an act of vandalism and illegal turned out to be an act of rescue and conservation. Life is full of contradictions. We used to sally forth with a huge, bushel-sized trug basket between us and a fern trowel. Orchis tubers are not generally deep at all, but we took no risks and dug each up surrounded by a good wodge of soil. It was the same with other orchids.

The so-called green-winged orchid has no green on it to warrant the name. It varies a lot in height, but is on average dwarfer than *Orchis mascula* and a cooler, less pink shade of purple. Another local orchid with which we are successful, and which flowers in May, is the twayblade, *Listera ovata*. It has two broad, opposite, basal leaves and a spike of perfectly green flowers. It is difficult to spot them in a largely green sward, but, once you've got your eye in, you'll realize that they are everywhere (where there are any!).

One thing I have learned is that you can expect to be able to naturalize the species that anyway grow wild in your locality, but not those that come from quite different habitats.

An enchanting little deciduous fern of undisturbed, permanent pasture puts in its appearance in spring: the adder's tongue, *Ophioglossum vulgatum*. Only a few centimetres tall, it has one glossy green leaf, like an arum's spathe, and this encloses the reproductive 'tongue', equivalent to an aroid's spadix.

Clovers are seldom included in seed mixtures recommended to those starting a meadow, because their nitrogen-fixing properties encourage just the kind of coarse, lush vegetation which you least want. But in an old, established meadow, clovers are very welcome and the red ones, really magenta, are out now, in force. They contrast with our three main species of buttercup. *Ranunculus bulbosus* is the first out; then the tall, widely branching meadow buttercup, *R. acris*, which has a neat double form, worthy of border space; third, the

creeping buttercup, *R. repens,* which can be a ferocious weed, in damp borders, spreading by overground stolons.

Moon daisies (or ox-eyed daisies), *Leucanthemum vulgare,* are an integral feature of a varied meadow turf, but I find that their populations come and go. In the upper moat, for instance, they used to be thick all over, but there are now scarcely any. This is a mystery; I believe that they get killed if there is a drought year, but there may be another reason. However, they spread into the garden proper and are a link between the wildness of the orchard and Lutyens's formal landscaping, where they invade the paving cracks in and around the circular steps. Red valerian, *Centranthus ruber,* is here, too, and in the terrace retaining walls overlooking the upper moat. I allow this invasion, joyfully, but as soon as the plants are fading, they receive a hard cut-back.

Top: One of the showiest additions to the meadows, this month, is the dazzling magenta *Gladiolus communis* subsp. *byzantinus.* We have to add it where we want it, as it does not set its own seed in our strain, but, once established, it persists. Here it is flourishing alongside Dutch *Iris* 'Blue Triumphator'.

Above: Red valerian thrives in the upper terrace wall above the upper moat meadow. I allow this invasion, joyfully, but as soon as the plants are fading, they receive a hard cut-back and order is restored.

Marginal planting

Our largest *Gunnera manicata* are in the partial shade of trees, by the lower moat. Their leaves are vast and visitors soon make a track through the long grass to have themselves photographed beneath a leaf. But most of the colour is out in the sun, by the horse pond. Here there are gunneras too, with the added interest of being conspicuously in flower. The multi-branched inflorescence could be compared with the scales of a fir cone but stands erect more obviously like a penis – a great attraction.

There are plenty of flowers, now, in and around the pond. On the banks, masses (too much, really) of the water dropwort, *Oenanthe crocata*, which is like a larger, more poised version of cow parsley, *Anthriscus sylvestris*, and lacks the latter's sickly flower scent. So it is good for cutting and arranging with its natural partner, also present in quantity and partly submerged, the wild *Iris pseudacorus*, with clear yellow flowers on 90cm/3ft stems.

Three other irises grow around here. In shallow water, one called 'Gerald Darby', with pale purple flowers on dark purplish stems. Then, also emergent, *I. versicolor*, which is principally reddish purple and white. The last species is *I. sibirica*, which is bluish purple. I have that in the high garden where I enjoy its colour contrast with

scarlet oriental poppies, but it is a dull dog, after flowering, and its lengthening leaves sprawl over the neighbours. In the margin of the pond, what it does after flowering passes unnoticed.

Happiest in water 30cm/1ft deep, or slightly more, is the golden club, *Orontium aquaticum*, which is a handsome aroid with sinuous flowering stems. Lacking the spathe of most aroids, it just produces a spadix, which is yellow at the tip and white behind it.

Underwater oxygenators can be terrible take-over plants but the well-behaved oxygenator which I really love is the so-called water violet, *Hottonia palustris*. It makes clouds of lacy foliage, arranged in loose rosettes, and appears throughout the winter dressed in bright green. In spring it may flower or it may not. The decision is probably dictated by how congested the colonies are.

If not congested, they flower, throwing up primula-like candelabrums of palest mauve blossom to about 30cm/1ft above the water. The display is very pretty.

There are willows on the bank between the pond and the forstal, which we pollard every third year. But at the bottom of them is a colony of the water saxifrage, *Darmera peltata*. Its rhizomes are right on the surface and it flowers, with domes of pink blossom on fleshy pink, hairy stems, before its umbrella leaves (like a mini-gunnera's) appear.

At times in its life, the lower moat in summer has been a continuous green sheet of duckweed, *Lemna* species. Now, we have none of that and I believe this to be on account of the 'wild' mallard (probably bred to be shot). Two or three of them spend much time here, and others on the horse pond. In spring, they try to breed, invariably without success, but they never give up.

Above: Water violet, *Hottonia palustris*, is an erratic flowerer.

Below: Golden club, *Orontium aquaticum*, is a particularly striking plant in the horse pond.

Im wunderschönen Monat Mai, als alle Knospen sprangen,
Da ist in meinem Herzen die Liebe aufgegangen.

(In the wonderful month of May, when all the buds burst open,
There love sprang up in my heart.)

Heine, Dichterliebe

Scents

On a bank set back from the horse pond is a deliciously scented shrub, which started flowering in April. This is *Elaeagnus umbellata*. It is not quite evergreen, losing the last of its old foliage in late winter. Now covered in young, greyish-green leaves together with thousands of tiny greenish flowers, it gives off this spicy aroma, which is carried on the wind into the high garden. Nearby, I also have the silver-leaved *E.* 'Quicksilver'. Its flowers are pale yellow, similarly scented, and they open a couple of weeks after the other's have finished. You should plant one or other of these near a sitting-out place. As a foliage plant, 'Quicksilver' is the better for earning its keep, but it is not so prolific a flowerer.

Among other notable scent-wafters, in May, is incense rose, *Rosa primula,* which has glandular foliage emitting this remarkable fragrance, especially after rain. The shrub is nothing much to look at. It congenitally suffers from dieback, as do others of these early, yellow-flowered roses – *R. xanthina* 'Canary Bird' and *R.x.* f. *hugonis,* for example – but it always recovers in the course of the summer. Another aromatic-leaved rose is the sweet briar, *R. rubiginosa,* at full stewed-apple strength on its young shoots.

Azara serrata is a vigorous evergreen shrub, which generally, for safety, needs to be grown against a sunny wall. That is smothered in bright yellow clusters of bloom, late in the month, and it smells strongly of fruit salad.

The May-flowering daphnes are night-scented and it's too chilly to be sitting out of an evening, so I should site them near a door which you have to go in and out of, even at night. The scent of *Daphne tangutica* is heavy, heady stuff, and this is one of the great survivors. Furthermore, it can be relied upon for a second crop, in the summer. The flowers are purplish on the outside, white within. I actually prefer *D. pontica,* which has rather smart lance leaves in loose rosettes. Its flowers are green and show up well – if you're looking for and at them. But their lemon scent is out of this world.

And the first of the climbing honeysuckles is out; they are night-scented. I have a particular weakness for *Lonicera caprifolium*. This is a pale honeysuckle and the leaves (or leaf-like bracts) below the flower cluster totally encircle the stem.

Wisteria sinensis flowers in the second half of May – some racemes earlier, if they lie against a warm wall. Although its racemes are of only moderate length, this is the best of wisterias, all round. Get yourself, from a reliable and accountable source, a vegetatively raised (not a seed-raised) clone. The clone that is still most often grown has been around since the early nineteenth

century and it usually has a second, light but welcome, crop of flowers in August. Mine is an old plant that was growing against the house, over a balcony and round a corner as far as the terrace doorway.

Another wisteria of which I am equally fond is *W. brachybotrys* 'Shiro-kapitan'. It has short racemes of well-spaced, large white flowers and the summery fragrance is the same and as good as in *W. sinensis*.

Persian lilac, *Syringa × persica* 'Alba', boasts glacier-white blossom; that is, white but with the faintest hint of bue. I prune out a lot of its flowered wood, immediately after flowering, and we also need to spray it against a fungal disease which attacks leaves and young stems. The public love it, and with good reason.

Permanent members of the borders

In this journal I touch on many incidentals in the mixed borders, especially the bulbs and bedders, but more needs to be said about their permanent contents. These are largely green, through May, and foliage is of great importance: for instance that of the cardoons, with their big, grey, deeply toothed leaves. The bright green foliage of oriental poppy, *Papaver orientale* Goliath Group, likewise lance-shaped and toothed, looks well in front of the cardoons. The poppy's huge red blooms, on upright, almost (but not dependably) self-supporting, 1.2m/4ft stems, are opening late in the month. Nearby, they flower in front of *Viburnum opulus* 'Compactum', which has white lacecaps.

One of the best leaves, before we have to surround it with a palisade of pea sticks, is that of *Clematis recta* 'Purpurea'. I think the scarlet type-plant of *Papaver orientale* looks super in front of that, in the high garden, but some would disagree (have done, in fact). But it pleases me and that, surely, is enough!

Splendid in its May dress is my clone of the ornamental rhubarb, *Rheum palmatum*. Its jagged-margined leaves are red-purple, on emerging, and remain purple on their undersides, which are still well displayed for several weeks. The flowers, by contrast, are white. All around this, I have late red tulips. The rheum is at the back of a deep

Moon daisies, *Leucanthemum vulgare*, red valerian and *Erigeron karvinskianus* have colonized the Lutyens circular steps.

border in the barn garden – because I want other plants to have grown up in front by the summer, when most of its leaves have died off. So I have a large patch, in front of it, of *Astilbe chinensis* var. *taquetii* 'Superba'. This has beautiful young foliage, pinnate, crimped and curled and rather hairy. All in among the astilbes we have established a self-sowing colony of the allium-like *Nectaroscordum siculum*, 90cm/3ft tall,

Self-sown plants

I should think a quarter of all the plants in the barn and sunk gardens are self-sowns whose seedlings we encourage, when they are in a suitable spot. Mostly, of course, they are not.

with umbels of bells in green and chestnut colouring. If isolated, this bulb can be rather a nuisance after flowering, but in with the astilbes it can do what it likes, disappearing in its own good time.

Libertias are out in May, with narrow, linear, evergreen leaves and white flowers that look triangular. *Libertia formosa* was my principal species in the wall garden/barn garden area, and it sows itself freely, sometimes in the steps dividing the two gardens. When near to *Euphorbia griffithii*, it makes a good contrast.

In one spot, *Libertia ixioides*, with its flowers spraying gracefully outwards, makes a nice companion behind the self-sown blue (nurseryman's blue) perennial cornflower, *Centaurea montana*, now in its first flush. After this, I cut the centaurea back and spray the resulting young shoots against mildew, and it flowers a second time in August.

In parts of the high garden, *Geranium yeoi* is a great unifying theme from late May till early July. It is biennial and has deeply cut foliage with red petioles. The flowers are like a glorified herb robert, *G. robertianum*, magenta-coloured. The trouble is that, if we leave too many of its seedlings, there is too great a gap when we need to pull it out in early July. We have successfully overcome this by threading plants (raised from seed in pots) of the ladybird poppy (red with

Fennel, *Ferula tingitana* 'Cedric Morris' towers above *Geranium* × *oxonianum* 'A.T. Johnson' and *Calamagrostis* × *acutiflora* 'Overdam' in the high garden.

black blotches) through the border where the geranium has been removed. Sun roses are flowering now, and at the front of one border there is *Helianthemum* 'Supreme' next to a white 'perennial' single stock and the geranium behind them. But this sort of combination is apt to change from year to year.

I am very fond of the stock, *Matthiola*, and it has the true stock scent. Under the right conditions, on light soil, it is a self-sower. But on a heavy soil like ours, it is uphill work. The leafy overwintering crown is apt to rot from botrytis.

There are several early-flowering geraniums flowering now. I have a particular fondness for *G. albanum*, which has nicely rounded flowers, quite close to the ground (unless there is a challenging neighbour for it to climb into), and of a chalk-pink colouring. When it has had its

Evening light casts delicate shadows from the long border.

turn, it dies back, so you can grow it among perennials that come into their own later in the season. In my case, these include *Hedychium densiflorum* (all hedychiums are late developers) and the giant reed grass, *Arundo donax,* in a position where I grow it right next to a path (for the sake of the distant view).

Then there is *Geranium × oxonianum* 'A.T. Johnson', which it is easy to have too

Lily-of-the-valley is one of those cussed plants that not only doesn't want to stay put, nor to grow where you'd like it to grow, but is inclined to take umbrage for no apparent reason.

much of because it is one of those ideal lazy gardener's ground-cover plants which covers the ground and flowers for months and months in a raucous shade of pinky mauve, getting increasingly untidy all the time.

If you get yourself in the right place, where several paths meet (two of them mud paths surrounding a stock bed), there is a good view of various plant shapes and colours: the geranium at your feet, shouting loudly; behind, a single clump of the variegated grass *Calamagrostis* × *acutiflora* 'Overdam' (this is a case where I believe that a singleton grass may be more telling than a group); a vivid 1.2m/4ft fennel, *Ferula tingitana* 'Cedric Morris', with shining green leaves and lime-green umbelliferous flower heads; in the distance, an excellent weigela, *Weigela* 'Praecox Variegata', thick with tubular blossom, now, of a more intense pink colouring than W. 'Florida Variegata'

and with a sharper leaf variegation. But I have the latter bang in the middle of the long border. The flowers are deliciously scented and I like their soft pink colouring with the pale yellow on their newly expanded leaves. Neither weigela turns dull, after flowering, as the green-leaved kinds do, so they earn their keep through to late autumn.

Elsewhere, the old-fashioned double crimson-red peony, *Paeonia officinalis* 'Rubra Plena', hangs over a carpet of London pride, *Saxifraga umbrosa,* a haze of tiny flesh-pink flowers. Behind these two, the white Portugal broom is in full bloom. I've kept that for very many years – for a broom – by conscientiously pruning it immediately after flowering.

Billowy tree lupins, *Lupinus arboreus,* now cover themselves with pale yellow spikes. Their sweet scent has none of the peppery quality of the perennial kinds.

Among the other essentials are lilies-of-the-valley, which I adore and should like to pick every stem of, for bunches to bring into the house or give away. That intermingles with the London pride and I must say its fortunes are chequered.

Iris tectorum is in the high garden. Its broad leaves are very fresh at its time of flowering and the flowers, with their huge, floppy standards, on quite short stems, are a lovely blue, which I far prefer to the albino.

Clematis

It is the season of *Clematis montana* and its many variants. Always be certain of equipping yourself with one that has the strong vanilla scent. This is often at its strongest when the flowers are almost over. My white *montana*, which was never a named clone but serves me excellently, is powerfully scented. The pale pink 'Elizabeth' is another winner.

'Marcel Moser' is similar to and of the same vintage (within a year) as 'Nelly Moser', but has longer sepals. Of course, it bleaches in the sun. Of the many more modern hybrids of similar appearance, 'Bees' Jubilee' has been a success and one specimen, planted inadvertently, is bountiful and regular as clockwork.

In the long border I have 'Lasurstern', a big blue, white-centred clematis that I've had for fifty years or more, either moved and divided or layered from its original position. This one was meant to grow over a *Viburnum* × *burkwoodii,* but I got tired of that, so the clematis now has to make do with pea sticks for support.

Clematis are all subject to wilt disease so Fergus drenches their roots with systemic fungicide (varying the ingredient, so that the fungi don't build up resistant strains). This eliminates trouble from powdery mildew, which afflicts many of the Texensis and Jackmanii hybrids later in the season.

One of my oldest clematis is 'Marcel Moser' growing up a post supporting the hovel roof, in the exotic garden (the old rose garden).

Other jobs for the month

Sowing and other propagating

O Make late sowings of tender annuals such as zinnias, quick-developing annuals like marigolds and cosmos, annuals to be used in the borders in July, and tender vegetables like cucumbers and gourds.

O Prick out seedlings once they are large enough to handle by their seed leaves.

O Sow most wallflowers, ahead of their flowering a year later. Wait until early July to sow the Siberian wallflower, *Erysimum linifolium,* otherwise they flower prematurely in the same year and the plants are weakened.

O Bring cannas and dahlias out from their winter quarters and check them carefully. Then take cuttings from dahlias if required.

Routine care

O Stake or in other ways support plants as they need it.

O Spray lupins, honeysuckles, viburnums, morello cherries, hellebores, shrubby euphorbias, cardoons and artichokes regularly against grey aphid, which can so quickly ruin them. Later, ladybirds or hoverfly larvae can help do the clearance job.

O Mark any rogue tulips as well as virus-infected, broken flowers, so they can be sorted out, later on, from the colour and variety that was intended.

Growing wallflowers

A lot can go wrong with this crop. It is not entirely hardy. It hates waterlogged conditions and in some pieces of ground, when growing on in a reserve area, it gets clubroot. We are now finding that the dwarf strains make large enough and more compact plants than the tall, and have gone over to them. When we bed out, I insist on close planting, with no gaps between units.

Tackling perennial weeds

There are certain perennial weeds that can never be got rid of but at least you can prevent them from getting worse: for example, a creeping vetch, *Vicia sepium,* which gets into paving cracks and also into the roots of other plants. Wearing rubber gloves and carrying a cup of ready-diluted Roundup, take a small paint brush or piece of sponge and apply this systemic herbicide on the weed's fresh leaves.

June

The ponds are tremendously lively, now.
There's no need for the tinkle of running
water to be aware of a pond and the wildlife
that congregates in and around it. Rising fish
make quite as much noise as I need and there
is a constant coming and going of birds.
Often, a blackbird nests in the dogwoods. It
skims low over the water as it goes to and fro
for food, and every time its shadow passes,
there's a scurrying swirl from disturbed and
scared fish. Of course we do get herons – one
heron at a time, because they are strictly
territorial. So I suppose a shadow could be a
threat. I'm glad to have the fish thinned
out a bit.

Early summer annuals and biennials

Herbaceous lupins make a grand display in early June. Their leaves are satisfying in the run-up to flowering and then the flower spikes themselves are an interesting combination of vertical and horizontal: upright spikes composed of horizontal whorls of flowers. Their warm, peppery scent is welcoming, too, and the sight of pollinating bees. However, after they have flowered, there is little you can do for lupins other than deadhead them. Occasionally they will be inspired to carry a worthwhile second crop, in July, but more often there'll be nothing on offer except mildewed foliage. So we sweep the lot away and replace with summer bedding.

Foxgloves have the same flowering season as lupins – I mean the biennial strains of our native *Digitalis purpurea*. We like the Glittering Prizes Group strain, with heavily spotted glove fingers, or the all-apricot-coloured strain. Foxgloves leave a gap after the end of June and we have to be ready to deal with that.

The double-flowered poppy strain *Papaver rhoeas* Angel's Choir Group has a great colour range only excluding the scarlet of field poppies, to which it would naturally revert. I also like the Turkish *P. tauricum*. These, and other members of the poppy family with exceedingly fragile roots, we sow in plugs, thinning the seedlings to one

Right: The one drawback to the growing of any lupin, such as these pink and yellow strains, beside *Weigela* 'Praecox Variegata', is the large and prolific grey aphid which so quickly ruins them, unless you are on the watch. We spray with something nasty, but one spraying is not enough. The aphids' waxy coating is highly resistant.

Below: We have made quite a June feature, in recent years, with the pure white umbellifer *Ammi majus* and a deep 'blue' larkspur, quite close to the wild type. I think *Consolida* 'Blue Cloud' is as near as you will get to it from a commercial source, but we save our own seed.

in each and planting them out without need of root disturbance. Those sown in March will flower in June and are excellent gap-fillers – for instance where forget-me-nots have been pulled out.

Both *Ammi majus* and our deep 'blue' wild larkspur are sown in the autumn and brought on in pots under cold glass. When grown this way, the ammi will reach a height of 1.8m/6ft, so the 90cm/3ft larkspur goes in front of that. Another good partner for ammi is the columns of willowy, fresh green leaves of *Helianthus salicifolius*, which we rate more important as a foliage rather than a flowering plant.

An annual/biennial that I dote on is the truly sky-blue *Cynoglossum amabile* (there are several obvious trade names). An early March sowing – or a September sowing if you can overwinter your stock under cold glass without its damping off – should have it in

An interesting experiment

Canterbury bells are naturally biennial. We sow them in April and either grow the seedlings on in pots or line them out for the summer like the lupins and foxgloves. One year, we planted out some not very large, pot-grown plants in autumn, interplanting them with *Lychnis* × *haageana*, grown on in pots from spring-sown seed. The main display was in June, but I deadheaded the bells as they turned brown, and this induced them to produce a very acceptable second crop. By that time, the lychnis had finished but we had made a direct sowing among them of the crimson-flowered annual *Papaver commutatum*, and that took over.

flower before the end of this month. We plant the cynoglossums out in April, or even May.

The clean cheerful orange of the annual daisy *Osteospermum hyoseroides* is a regular feature at Dixter, as Fergus and I are both so keen on it. This is quick-maturing and you don't want to keep it waiting if, following a spring sowing and individual potting, it is ready to go out.

St John's Day being 24 June, *Anthemis sancti-johannis* is so named for flowering at that time. We find this to be best treated like a biennial. It is the cleanest, most uncompromisingly orange daisy imaginable (needing twig support, even though only 60cm/2ft tall) and I love it in the long border with the magenta *Geranium psilostemon*. We may tone these down with apricot foxgloves and 'blue' larkspurs.

Of rather similar habit are the florists' pyrethrums, *Tanacetum coccineum*, and they have a great freshness, in June. We like the crimson, yellow-centred kinds and the seed strain is listed as Robinson's red-flowered. We sow in the spring of the previous year and line the plants out to grow on, but as they hate disturbance in autumn, we do not move them into their flowering quarters till the early spring. They are already showing new growth in February.

Salvia sclarea is a bold, upstanding biennial, 90–120cm/3–4ft sage with an

Right: I thought *Eryngium giganteum* looked pretty good in front of my old colony of *Melianthus major*, now just getting under way after being cut to the ground at winter's end.

Below: *Osteospermum hyoseroides* mixes well with blue, for instance the annual woodruff-related *Asperula orientalis* (which is one of the few blue-flowered umbellifers) or with the bulbous *Triteleia laxa* (as here).

inflorescence of mauve flowers and rosy-mauve bracts. On light soils it is self-perpetuating but on our clay we need to raise it under controlled conditions. Which we gladly do, as plants with a presence such as this are invaluable and it has a long season.

I like *Lychnis coronaria* in front of it. This comes into its own at the end of the month, with stiffly branching grey stems (and leaves) supporting a 75cm/2½ft structure with brilliant magenta, moon-shaped flowers. It is a self-sower and although technically perennial, it is at its best in its second year from seed and should never be kept beyond a third. It creates a range of daring combinations for itself. Less abrasive but equally effective, this month, is its positioning in front of the bright green foliage of *Grevillea* 'Canberra Gem', which is an evergreen asset year-round.

Those of us with long-established gardens are sure to have *Eryngium giganteum*, known as Miss Willmott's ghost. But we depend on its self-sowing, as its taproot makes it an unsatisfactory subject for raising in pots and planting out. And so, each year, it will be somewhere different from where it was last. Starved plants may not flower for several years but under good conditions it should be biennial.

The June gap
Between the removal of spring bedding and the settling in of its summer replacements, we plant June-flowering biennials or early summer perennials treated as biennials.

The best of Dixter in June

The perennials

It is, or should be, impossible to discuss perennials without at the same time including some shrubs and other categories of plants, since they all help each other. And, of course, bulbs are perennials.

What are penstemons? Soft shrubs, really, and at winter's end, I either cut the old plants hard back, to sprout more vigorously from low down, or I leave them to flower a little earlier on the growth they brought through the winter. A third alternative is to start them again each year from cuttings, taken late in the summer of the previous year. This gives the most level results. I like the combination of *Penstemon* 'Drinkstone Red', which is a soft shade of red, with the rich purple spikes of *Salvia* × *superba* and the flat heads of a pale yellow achillea. 'Moonshine' has nice grey foliage but the yellow is a bit too bright. I prefer the sport from *A*. 'Taygetea' that turned up in my own garden and which I called 'Lucky Break'; this grows to 90cm/3ft and is a soft though distinct yellow.

The salvia has great staying power and, being a sterile hybrid, can be relied upon to flower a second time in September. Similar at a lower level, in June, though with no great tendency to flower a second time, is *Salvia nemorosa* 'Ostfriesland'. That would be a suitable companion for *Anthemis sancti-*

The vibrant colours in the stock beds here include *Penstemon* 'Drinkstone Red', *Salvia* × *superba*, *Achillea* 'Lucky Break', *Verbascum chaixii* and *Cynara cardunculus.*

johannis. The anthemis that is now coming into its own is the pale yellow *A. tinctoria* 'Wargrave Variety'. Quite by accident, it flowered with *Yucca gloriosa* 'Nobilis', with an impressive candelabrum of waxy, cream bells. This yucca is less stiff than ordinary *Y. gloriosa* and it has an interesting bluish cast. Also, it is less inclined to flower out of season, which is an advantage, as you can plan accordingly.

This is the month for old-fashioned pinks – *Dianthus plumarius* and its many hybrids. I always grow a batch of *D.* 'Rainbow Loveliness', treated as a biennial, and that has a deliciously sweet scent on the air, but it is not the typical pink scent. Its seed ripens in late July and we sow it forthwith for flowering the next year. I also grow the carnation-like (though classified as a pink) 'Haytor's White', which is neatly double, is scented and flowers over quite a long season.

Rejuvenating anthemis

Anthemis tinctoria, and others of the same genus, may grow inconveniently tall, to 1.2m/4ft, on older plants, needing a lot of support; and they are subject to powdery mildew. Then, suddenly, the whole colony exhausts itself and you may find that there's nothing left for next year. The solution I adopt is to take soft cuttings from its mossy young basal growth in February. These, potted individually, will be ready to use as bedding plants by May, and they will flower non-stop from late June till late autumn, given just one deadheading. No mildew and just one cane and a tie for each plant is sufficient.

I don't really go in for the early-flowering kniphofias but a super form of *Kniphofia caulescens* given me by Helen Dillon does flower in June, although September is the normal flowering time for the most widely distributed clone. Helen's has the usual coral-coloured flowers but its chief excellence resides in its amazingly bold leaf rosettes, which are the expected glaucous colouring. My plant makes an arresting corner feature and it has *Trochodendron aralioides* behind it, now in flower. The flowering panicles of this are fresh, bright green and their main feature is a circle of stamens which look like the spokes of a wheel (*trochos* is Greek for a wheel).

On another nearby corner, the feature is a clump of *Stipa gigantea*, now flowering; a grass which ideally lends itself to an important position of this kind. It makes a 1.8m/6ft fountain of oat-like flowering

panicles, which are rose-tinted while young and last until high winds blow them to bits in the autumn. This is a see-through plant. From the lower terrace you can look through the stipa to the tall 'blue' panicles of *Campanula lactiflora,* coming into its own at the end of the month. Beyond that a view of two tall clumps of giant reed grass, *Arundo donax,* with glaucous leaves.

Many campanulas are at their peak in June. *Campanula persicifolia,* whether white or blue, is a great self-sower; our heavy soil suits it to perfection. As it is shade-tolerant, it often sows itself under a hedge or shrub and then peers out from that at a height of 60cm/2ft or so. The blue version would combine well with *Pimpinella major* 'Rosea', a 90cm/3ft, June-flowering umbellifer – native, but quite insignificantly white in the wild, whereas a fairly intense pink strain is a very good colour indeed.

I suppose *Allium cristophii* is just about the best species for general garden purposes. It has large globes of stiff, lilac-mauve segments, and these persist, so that even when the colour fades the globe retains its presence for a long time. I am pleased with it among Japanese anemones. It peps them up before their season but does them no harm.

Allium moly, only 23cm/9in tall, is bright yellow. Its display is brief but it is a good

Allium cristophii is the sort of perennial that can be fitted into many places, such as among *Geranium* 'Ann Folkard' and *Salvia nemorosa* 'Ostfriesland'. Given a start, it will go on with the good work by self-sowing.

filler between the bottom of yew topiary and the adjacent lawn. Among it, we have a self-sown spotted orchid, *Dactylorhiza fuchsii.* With its mauve spikes this works so well that I shall make an intentional planting with more of it. The natural hybrid *D.* × *grandis* is larger and more important-looking, therefore deserving border space, which I have lately given it.

June is a great month for cistus. One of the most persistent and long-lived is also my favourite, *Cistus* × *cyprius.* Its large white blooms, a fresh crop each morning, have a maroon blotch at the base of each petal. But the leaves are also interesting: a dark, solemn green with a touch of blue in them which, in cold weather, may be heightened to the colour of lead. The bush grows to 1.8m/6ft and has a lax habit, so that it leans on its elbows. It can grow as it pleases and can do no wrong in my sight. It is apt to

Solo performers

In a fairly shady barn garden border, we have a good colony (which Fergus replants every other year) of the dragon arum, *Dracunculus vulgaris* (see above left). In spring, its speckled shoots look like a team of adders disappearing underground. In fact they are emerging and expand into fascinating leaves, constructed on the same principle as *Helleborus foetidus* and *Adiantum pedatum* (see above right), with leaflets radiating from an arc. The large purple arum flowers open late in the month and on the first day smell of carrion, which attracts pollinating bluebottles. After that the smell subsides, each bloom lasting for three days. The total display is brief but a great event.

harbour weeds in its depths, which demand a grovel to extract.

Under a deciduous escallonia, I have a colony of the evergreen *Saxifraga stolonifera*, which is an overground runner with loose rosettes of scalloped, hairy leaves beautifully marked in different shades of green. To everyone's surprise, that bursts into flower in June, with open sprays of lopsided white blossom, about 30cm/1ft high.

This is at one end of the north-west-facing bed with heavy soil where I had a January display of snowdrops. They have now been displaced by its perennial contents. There's a vigorous form of *Rodgersia pinnata* freely producing 90cm/3ft panicles of blossom in a good shade of pink. In front of it, I have *Geranium wallichianum* 'Buxton's Variety', which will not start flowering till next month but whose sharply jagged and well-marked foliage is already an asset. Behind

these, *Euphorbia palustris,* now fading, and *Aralia cachemirica,* with boldly pinnate leaves and still coming on.

One of the brightest features at the horse pond's margin is Bowles's golden sedge, *Carex elata* 'Aurea', and it retains a good colour till August. This is also an excellent border plant, where the soil is damp, and contrasts effectively with hosta and rodgersia leaves. But don't plant it in shade, or much of its brilliance will be lost.

There are wild honeysuckles around the horse pond, one of them overhanging the water, another twining up an oak sapling which we pollard, but, for the sake of the woodbine, not too hard. Many of the wild honeysuckles seed themselves around the garden. One has reached to the top of the bay tree, and there is another growing over a *Cotoneaster horizontalis* in the sunk garden. The late Dutch honeysuckle *Lonicera periclymenum* 'Serotina' has particularly rich dark red buds. I grow that on a pole close to the house and it is fully out by the end of June.

Another wilding with garden selections is the common elder, *Sambucus nigra.* As a bush it is fairly nondescript, but in flower it is transformed, every branch being lined, on its upper side, with flat corymbs of cream-white, scented blossom. In the garden, we grow two kinds for their blossom. The earlier is *S.n.* f. *porphyrophylla* 'Guincho Purple', with purple leaves and fairly small flower heads in which the anthers are pink, so the inflorescence is slightly flushed. The cut-leaved *S.n.* f. *laciniata* is the other and that has particularly large flower heads.

The elder I grow entirely for foliage, giving it a hard cut-back all over, in winter, is *S.n.* 'Marginata'. It has a broad marginal variegation, pale yellow maturing to white.

Growing about 45cm/18in tall, *Cynoglossum amabile* mixes well, in a harmony that should soothe the most easily shattered nerves, with the young glaucous foliage of blue lyme grass, *Leymus arenarius.*

Peacock garden

There is quite an event, late in June, in the peacock garden (see below), where the topiary peacocks are linked by double hedges of the bushy Michaelmas daisy, *Aster lateriflorus* var. *horizontalis*. Between these double rows I have ribbons of a purple English iris, *Iris latifolia*, the last of all the bulbous irises to flower. Its foliage can die off here unnoticed, being concealed within the asters' growth. If you look across to the house from this area, you'll see a white 'Kiftsgate' rose flowering in the branches of a damson plum. And you'll be struck by its scent, if you approach a little nearer. We make an effort to prune this each winter, removing the previous year's flowered growths. If you don't do this, the whole thing becomes an uncontrolled monster and will soon bring its support crashing to the ground.

Wall garden

The highlight for me now and till the autumn is *Paris polyphylla*. It grows in a shady border in the wall garden and you might not notice it at first, since it is green in the midst of a lot more green – the filigree lady fern, *Athyrium filix-femina* 'Plumosum Axminster', is one striking neighbour (see below). The paris rises 60cm/2ft on a naked stem and there produces a whorl of lance leaves. Next come the floral parts, also in whorls, finally crowned by a central knob, which is the developing ovary. This amazing structure is all in muted shades of yellow (the stamens), purple and green. The ovary gradually enlarges and splits open in October to reveal brilliant orange seeds.

Every ferula has wonderful filigree foliage and all are different. The one most grown here is *F. communis*, and this, with its lime-green blossom, now reaches 2.4m/8ft.

The trouble with June is the speed with which it flashes by. Everything is coming to maturity, but is still young and fresh.

Wild flowers

In the meadow areas the wild flowers reach a climax, this month. They are dominated by yellow daisies, of which there are several species but the commonest is *Leontodon autumnalis*, the autumnal hawkbit, which flowers from June to October. To see its display at its best, you have to catch it right. The flowers are not fully open till mid-morning and they follow the sun, so you need to have the sun behind you. By early afternoon the flowers are closing. This has seeded itself into the topiary garden lawns in a big way, since I started to let them grow long, a few years ago. The topiary pieces, themselves shaggy with young growth, seem to be swimming in the deep sward and there is much white clover, conveying its honeyed fragrance.

Here, and elsewhere in the poorest soil, the dominant grass is common bent and that flowers at the end of June and in early July, a lovely soft pink, though much paler on dewy mornings. (Rather similar, at a higher level, is the impression made by a couple of smoke bushes, *Cotinus coggygria*, which become hazy immediately after flowering, pink at first but easily dew-laden.)

Wild orchids, whose seeds are so light, are moving in without assistance, but the early part of this month sees wonderful displays of spotted orchids, *Dactylorhiza fuchsii*, in its principal self-appointed

Autumn hawkbit, clover and buttercups prevail in the meadows.

strongholds. These are in the orchard, in the prairie, which was once an orchard, and in the shady hollow next to the forstal (where, also, there is a late, heavily fragrant azalea, *Rhododendron arborescens*, flowering). The orchid's spikes are dense and in varying shades of mauve, some so intense that they would be worth selecting, if I could be bothered.

My mother, who used to raise them from seed, added meadow cranesbills, *Geranium pratense,* to a number of areas and that is as good a blue as you'll find in any cranesbill. Then there is the indigo-purple *Iris latifolia*, of whose role in the peacock garden I wrote earlier. Whenever we replant this, there is masses of surplus stock and we find that it is perfectly able to maintain itself under competitive meadow conditions, flowering well in some years, poorly in others, but totally undemanding.

Water lilies

The water lilies such as *Nymphaea* 'Rose Arey' (see below) are all in bloom, now. They are not fully open much before 11 a.m., and by 3 p.m. on a hot day the water lilies may already have started to close, though it will be an hour later in less fierce weather.

I have some half-dozen varieties. As I don't want them to mix and as I also always want to be able to see plenty of the water's surface, I get a water garden specialist to come each year and relieve me of stock around the perimeter of each colony. Most of mine are crimson or a reasonably strong shade of pink but I have lately added an exciting yellow called *N.* 'Texas Dawn'. Its flowers present themselves several centimetres above the water's surface – during the first day or two, that is. On the third day they sink back to the surface and on the fourth they're done.

Other jobs for the month

Planting

O Settle on how to arrange plantings of dahlias and cannas and of exotica that have overwintered under heated glass – cacti, succulents, streptocarpus, foliage begonias and many other exciting foliage plants.

Dealing with produce

O Harvest spinach, early calabrese and the first ambrosial flush of globe artichokes.

O Freeze green gooseberries while they are still on the small side.

Routine care

O As soon as you see first colour in raspberries, spray against the raspberry beetle, whose maggots would otherwise spoil a dish of the ripe fruit.

O Check for sawfly caterpillars on gooseberries and redcurrants.

O Line out lupin seedlings for next year to grow on in a reserve area.

O Cut *Eucalyptus gunnii* back hard to keep its growth in the attractive juvenile state if it has a good blue colouring.

O Hard prune the pink-variegated box elder, *Acer negundo* 'Flamingo', to encourage it to go on producing new young foliage, which has the colour, through summer.

O Pull away old leaves from *Yucca gloriosa* and phormiums. Steady the plant with your other hand as you do this, otherwise there's the risk of losing an entire branch.

O Prune cut-leaved sumach, *Rhus glabra* 'Laciniata', paulownias and *Ailanthus altissima* back to ground level, so as to procure the largest leaves possible on their young growth.

O Continue routine mowing and edging, staking, weeding and irrigating, if necessary.

Lupins

We like to choose two single-colour seed strains, grow them separately and then mix them when bedding out in the autumn. Thus, we might have pink and yellow one year, yellow and blue another, or blue and red in a third. It should, of course, be understood that the modern lupin often already combines two colours in each flower – the top half, for instance, may be blue and the bottom half white. This adds to the excitement. Total mixtures of colours, which are the easiest to obtain from the seed merchants, are all right in their way, but it is good to be able to exercise some colour control.

July

This is the climax month of the year for flowering plants as also for many insects. Butterflies, alas, are in pretty short supply, these days. But there are masses of meadow browns, with their floppy flight, and towards the end of July the annual hatch of peacocks is suddenly with us. Large and small whites are about and migrate in greater or lesser numbers from the continent, not only paying attention to our brassicas but quickly decimating nasturtiums. Seakale, stocks and cleomes are other favourite foods.

Hydrangeas

Some hydrangeas are particularly rewarding because of their long-flowering season. *Hydrangea macrophylla* 'Madame Emile Mouillère' is one of these; a white hortensia, already flowering early in the month. As the flowering heads become unsightly, sometime in September, you remove the branches carrying them and the display continues on the young shoots, often even into November, if frost holds off.

Another with a long season is *H.m.* 'Ayesha', a hortensia which is medium pink with me and is distinguished from all others (to date) by its incurving florets. This needs a sheltered wall position in order to flower freely and I have it so that the eye takes it in together with *Buddleja* 'Dartmoor', with its heavy multiple panicles of light purple blossom hanging over the wall from behind it. 'Ayesha' flowers on and on, provided that it brings its old wood through the winter. In that case, it will flower both on the old wood and on the new. If it doesn't, it will be so busy making new wood that this will be too soft and sappy to flower at all and will become an easy victim to the next winter's frosts.

I am fond of many of the lacecaps, too, and I think they mix perfectly well with hortensias, if you want them to. Of the other, really winter-tough kinds of hydrangea, an outstanding example that comes into its own late in the month is *H. arborescens*

Hydrangeas and soil

Hydrangeas like moisture; they do not like too alkaline a soil but if, like ours, it is neutral or thereabouts, you have the opportunity of obtaining a rich red colour from those, like *Hydrangea macrophyla* 'Westfalen' (a hortensia – that is, bun-headed) or *H.m.* 'Möwe' (a lacecap) which will give it to you. On really acid soils, they will inevitably be deep blue.

If your soil is sort of in-between, you can quite easily (though with some labour) convert it to a sufficiently acid condition with weekly waterings with a solution of aluminium sulphate. Or you can spread the crystals over the ground above the plants' roots and thoroughly dissolve them from a hose or watering can. Do this from about late February till the flower buds are colouring. Within a couple of years, it will be working a treat. However, if you want a good strong pink or red and it is apt to be muddy mauve, a lime dressing will operate in the opposite direction.

Hydrangeas are enlivened by the giant reed grass
Arundo donax and foreground plants.

'Annabelle'. It flowers on its young wood and can therefore be pruned quite hard back each winter. But if you prune it too hard, the young shoots will bear enormous bunheads on rather weak stems, which will flop. So we leave (or I leave – Fergus enjoys a hard pruning) some growth on last year's stronger young shoots to carry the smaller flower heads. In either case, we find it advisable to provide some support (discreet, of course). 'Annabelle' is pure white and can be excessively dominant if placed in a too prominent position. So I have learned to site it at the back of the long border. Even though it grows only 1.2m/4ft high, it makes a quite sufficient impression from there, and doesn't jump at you prematurely. It fades gracefully and when bleached to beige is one of the good features in the border's early winter aspect.

Life in the meadows

Water and meadow

The horse pond area is as lively as ever and the main water lily feature is *Nymphaea* 'James Brydon', with a season not as long as some of the others but generous while it lasts. Its full, bowl-shaped flowers, between pink and purple, are striking. Yellow continues to be supplied by marginal brooms, mostly of the wild kind, *Cytisus scoparius*. The weight of blossom brings their branches down to, even into, the water. With the added impact of their reflections, the display is quite something.

There is quite a free-for-all growth of vegetation over much of the sunk garden floor, almost like a meadow, at this stage, before we have attempted to impose order. The young burrs on *Acaena novae-zelandiae* turn brilliant carmine, in July, and contrast with the yellow of self-introduced bird's-foot trefoil, *Lotus corniculatus*. But I have also introduced a plant of *Spiraea japonica* 'Anthony Waterer', which gives a little height, while its own flowers are the same colour as the acaena's burrs. Very tall, here, and in many parts of the barn garden, above, are self-sown *Oenothera glazioviana*. Its name keeps changing but it is the one with by far the largest yellow flowers. They do not open till well after sunset but continue in good condition the next day, until mid-morning, especially if the weather is dull.

There are plenty of teasels now flowering. This starts as a narrow band of mauve around the centre of the green cone. It divides and becomes two bands, one moving upwards, one down. It is a strange performance. And throughout the summer, the biennial *Euphorbia stricta* displays its open sprays of pale green flowers.

A speciality in this garden is another biennial, *Centaurium erythraea*, the common

> ### *Houttuynia cordata* 'Chameleon'
>
> In the sunk garden pond, I have a pot of *Houttuynia cordata* 'Chameleon'. It is perfectly happy in shallow water and its amazing pink, yellow and green colouring is much heightened in a sunny position and where it is a little starved through root restriction. In a border, it is so rampant as to present something of a problem. We do have it at the top of the long border, but Fergus has had to prevent (or try to prevent) its progress into border neighbours with a vertical strip of metal, sunk into the ground.

centaury. It belongs to Gentianaceae and the rosette of leaves that it makes in its first year is uncommonly reminiscent of the rosettes in *Gentiana acaulis*. In its second, it rises to 30cm/1ft with an open corymb of bright pink, star-like flowers which only open out in sunshine. A joyful little plant.

But to return for a moment to the principal meadow areas: their shaggy appearance does not in the least irk me (it does some), except where wet weather has laid the grass. That only happens where the soil is richer than it should be and in a fiendish season of wind and rain. The wild flower that cheers us up all through the month is the tufted vetch, *Vicia cracca*, which is an excellent shade of blue. In the dampness of the bottom of the upper moat, meadow sweet, *Filipendula ulmaria,* is bearing its creamy flower heads.

Among July's perennials

Crocosmia 'Lucifer' is flowering best in the second half of July and is soon joined, at a lower level, by the bright but pleasing yellow *Coreopsis verticillata*. This has a stiff habit but its stems are thin and wiry and the foliage filigree fine.

By now, we are right into the prime season for yellow daisies, most notably, at Dixter, with *Inula magnifica*. This grows to 2m/7ft and carries easily branching candelabrums with notably long-rayed daisies, the rays quivering individually when there is a breeze. It makes a good border plant; as it starts late into growth, the widely separated clumps are interplanted with tulips. But it looks even better in one corner of the orchard where there is a concentration of poet's narcissus. Here we grow a very widely spaced colony of inula clumps which make solo features and are yet members of their community.

Inula hookeri is quite different but a favourite in its own way. It has a rhizomatous habit and makes a colony which needs controlling. Although only 90cm/3ft high, it does benefit from support. Its buds show the rays twisted in a spiral before they unfold and they are very fine, the yellow soft, as bright yellows go, and this is enormously popular with butterflies.

Senecio doria is a part of the grand display at the top of the long border, so I will

Strongly structured perennials are at a premium. Among them is Veratrum album, *a perennial having a tendency to flower freely one year and scarcely at all in another.*

Opposite: Between the scarlet of *Crocosmia* 'Lucifer' and the yellow of *Coreopsis verticillata*, I want a sandwich of soothing blue sea holly, *Eryngium × oliverianum*, which is just about the best of its kind with sizeable blue flower heads and incredibly metallic blue stems.

Below: At the end of the long border are *Verbascum olympicum*, *V. chaixii*, *Clematis* 'Jackmanii Superba', *Hoheria lyallii* and *Senecio doria*.

deal with a lot of that in one big mouthful. It is self-supporting, 1.8m/6ft tall, with flat heads of small, bright yellow daisies, not unlike a ragwort's but the leaves are smooth, undivided and shiny. It is contrasted behind with a column of purple *Clematis* 'Jackmanii', trained up a long chestnut pole. That is at the back of the border and to one side of it is the white, cherry-like blossom of a New Zealand shrub, *Hoheria glabrata*.

A lot of yellow around here is contributed by the random planting and self-sowing of two verbascum. The perennial *Verbascum chaixii* (1.2m/4ft) has narrow, sparsely branching spikes of small yellow flowers which are surprisingly highlighted by purple stamens. The biennial *V. olympicum* (2m/7ft) we have a great deal of between here and the high garden. It makes a heavy candelabrum (we need to give each plant a stake), which branches generously near the top, making a powerful head of yellow bloom. In the orchard garden, next above the long border, it looks splendid on a bank with yew hedging for a background and it mixes well (I think) there, with red hollyhocks. All verbascums wilt in hot sunshine, so they need to be enjoyed before 11 a.m.

There's a satisfying hebe/cranesbill combination in the high garden, but with the addition of the pale grey stems of *Artemisia ludoviciana* 'Silver Queen'. This grows into a bush of *Hebe* 'Watson's Pink'. After a series of mild winters, this is now 1.8m/6ft tall and on its other side the 'blue' *Clematis* 'Prince Charles' has a handhold. The hebe is now smothered in short spikes of clear pink blossom. Pink and grey obviously go well together. Another strong colour here is the harsh purple *Verbena rigida*. The fact that its flower heads and flowers are small makes the strength of its colouring necessary.

At last, the evenings and nights have ceased to be chilly and it is right for picnics and taking our evening drinks to the top of the long border. About seven of us can fit on to Lutyens's seat. It has two return bits at the ends and the one nearest the orchard gives you the best view of the long border itself, but in the gloaming it is just as good to be looking towards the sunset sky, against which the ash trees are silhouetted.

Summer shrubs

I want to include some shrubs which don't especially fit into my community plantings. For instance, the very first thing you see on arriving at Dixter, in July, is a mature *Genista aetnensis*, the Mount Etna broom. It is growing in meadow turf, whose competitive nature made the broom's early progress extremely slow (and I am trying to establish others, in this area, which are having the same difficulties). But once away, this is the longest-living broom species, giving you thirty years or more. It is almost a tree, at maturity, with very thin, raining branches. They are green and do all, or nearly all, the photosynthesizing; tiny leaves are soon shed. Short flower spikelets occur at the tips of every new shoot, so this becomes a fragrant fountain of yellow, for some three weeks.

By contrast, the other summer-flowering broom, *Spartium junceum*, from the Mediterranean, is stiff and large-flowered, though again on terminal spikes and even more sweetly and heavily scented. It is no elegant beauty but a great performer and its bright, clean shade of yellow is peculiarly satisfying. I grow quite a number, but would specially like to mention *Cistus × pulverulentus* 'Sunset'. It is fairly low-growing with sage-green leaves and vivid magenta flowers over an exceptionally long period.

There is a satisfying group in the high garden. At the back is hard-pruned shrub *Catalpa bignonioides* 'Aurea, with its nice big leaves at or just above eye level. In front of that is the arborescent form of ivy, *Hedera helix* f. *poetarum* 'Poetica Arborea'. At 1.8m/6ft, it has grown larger than I expected or wished, but the catalpa still gives it the right background. By its side, quite low (60cm/2ft) *H.h.* 'Buttercup' is such a bright yellow that it tends to scorch in hot sunshine.

Of some importance as a corner feature in the high garden are several interlocking plants of *Hebe* 'Pewter Dome'. It is a dense evergreen with greyish foliage, entirely obliterated just now with spikelets of white flowers, whose anthers are contrasting black – always a pedigree point, like the black anthers in some white agapanthus or the black tongue in a chow.

One of the few shrubby umbellifers, *Bupleurum fruticosum*, bears lime-green inflorescences. It is a cornerpiece in the L-shaped border in front of the house, and has our main bedding-out ideas in front of it. The shrub is a handsome evergreen, but apt to become over-large and unwieldy. Or, if you clip it over in spring, it becomes smugly rotund. However, I find that it can be cut to stumps, in spring, and will joyfully react in the same season with young shoots up to 1.8m/6ft long. It flowers and flowers and

flowers and, if you sow its seeds absolutely fresh, can be easily increased that way.

Yet another lime-greener, grown against a south wall in the wall garden, is *Cestrum parqui*, whose first burst of blossom – panicles of small, tubular flowers opening into stars at the mouth – generally occurs throughout this month if it carried some of last year's wood alive through the winter. If it did not, it has to start again from ground level and will not flower till August. After a July flowering, there will be a second, equally generous crop in autumn. The plant's and flowers' normal smell is rather sour, as in many of the Solanaceae, but at night there is a transformation, with a delicious almond scent on the air.

In the wall garden, I grow the yellow-leaved form of white poplar, *Populus alba* 'Richardii', for its foliage – pollarding it hard.

Other jobs for the month

Replanting

O Remove any fading plants and replace with fresh ones, to keep the interest going for another three months.

O If the plants, like alstroemerias or delphiniums, can't be moved out, tuck in annual climbers to grow over their skeletons, notably blue ipomoeas, with little sheaves of tubular flowers in orange, yellow and white.

Dealing with the produce

O Gather all the good things coming in from the garden – they may need to be dealt with in rather a hurry.

O Freeze broad beans and green peas while still young and tender (and before the beans are wearing tough jackets).

O Pick raspberries; 'Malling Delight' are too large and squishy for preserving.

O Make jelly from any redcurrant bushes.

O Use blackcurrants in various ways.

July replacement plants

We largely depend on cannas, dahlias or bedders raised from late-sown seed. We also lean quite heavily on nasturtiums, and there'll be some tuberous-rooted begonias, excellent for rather shady places. We have got the hang of and enjoy growing *Coleus* (now *Solenostemon*) hybrids for bedding; a May sowing brings the plants on very handily to be used as replacements for other bedding in early July. Late-sown zinnias and *Tithonia rotundifolia* 'Torch', which is like a zinnia but brilliant orange and up to 1.8m/6ft tall, are good standbys. Also *Ricinus*, the castor oil bean, for its handsome foliage. There are several strains.

August

There are heavy dews at night. The yew
hedges have yet to be trimmed (that starts
in the last week) and they are hung with dew-
laden cobwebs. The countryside around now
looks tired and tarnished, the trees, especially
the oaks, heavy and brooding. But the garden
is an oasis of voluptuous luxuriance. It may
pant and go limp in the early afternoon heat
but for most of the time it flaunts, yet in a
contented sort of way. Fergus and I revel in
this season and the many opportunities that
it provides. We have been planning for it right
through the year and we continue to plan
and prepare for September and October.

The exotic garden

Cannas and other high colour

Besides dahlias, cannas are the other great contributors to the general excitement of the Dixter exotic garden, as much for their leaves as for their bundles of silken flowers. The latter are greatly at the mercy of the weather and you need to go over them frequently, removing dead blooms – they just pull off.

Two of the liveliest for their variegated leaves are *Canna* 'Striata', which is striped in green and yellow, and 'Phasion', which is stripily variegated in rich shades of pink. Both hold their leaves more or less upright and greatly benefit from back-lighting. Both have orange flowers.

The best orange-flowered canna is 'Wyoming' (1.8m/6ft or more), which has purple foliage and goes splendidly with *Dahlia* 'David Howard'. An excellent purple-leaved variety called *Canna* 'General Eisenhower' looks like a piece of bronze sculpture, before it flowers (1.2m/4ft), and the flowers are pure red. Its vigour is only moderate, which can be an advantage. My most vigorous and prolific canna is *C. indica* 'Purpurea' (1.8m/6ft). It has fairly narrow purplish leaves and small orange-red flowers. Having the largest (purplish) leaves is the well-named *C.* 'Musifolia' (1.8m/6ft) and we grow that entirely for its banana-like foliage, as it has never flowered yet.

There are many more good plants in this garden and it is always in a state of flux, as we are always experimenting.

I like to grow red lobelias in the exotic garden. They peak this month. *Lobelia cardinalis* 'Queen Victoria' (90cm/3ft) has purple stems and leaves and big spikes of pure, volcanic red flowers. It is a non-branching plant that needs support halfway up its stems. Again, a fine companion for the white-variegated grass *Arundo donax* var. *versicolor*. These lobelias make basal rosettes of foliage wherewith to overwinter but should be given protection. Bedding them into a frame is generally sufficient and they can be split to keep them healthy, in the spring.

A general stir is caused by the various angel's trumpets of the genera *Datura* and the larger, woodier *Brugmansia* (which used to be lumped into *Datura*). *Datura inoxia* (75cm/2½ft) makes a bushy plant and is generally treated as an annual – by us, anyway. Its white funnel flowers face

The exotic garden includes plenty of lush foliage setting off the dahlias.

upwards. They open at dusk and are worth watching as they do it, in a rapid series of jerks. They are heavily fragrant on the first evening.

We cut back and house the brugmansias, in winter, and grow them to 1.5–1.8m/5–6ft, so that we can readily admire their large, pendent bells. The white *B. suaveolens* is best known and we also have the rather nice buff-coloured 'Grand Marnier'. Both are heavily fragrant. But, in both, the large, coarse leaves are totally undistinguished. I can easily forget and forgive that fault.

The ginger relatives of the genus find a home here, having good foliage as well as interesting flowers. *Hedychium densiflorum* 'Assam Orange' (75cm/2½ft) has dense spikes of small orange flowers. In *H. greenii* (90cm/3ft) the main feature is the shining bronze undersides to the leaves. The flowers are red, but cannot be relied upon to put in an appearance. This is one of the less hardy species.

We have some favourites at ground level. Tuberous-rooted begonias, for instance, especially small-flowered scarlet 'Flamboyant'. Also, yellow-flowered *Oxalis spiralis* subsp. *vulcanicola*, a ground-coverer which could become a ferocious weed, were it not frost-tender. Then, the delightful little prostrate *Impatiens pseudoviola*, which has a long succession of white, violet-like flowers.

Foliage in the exotic garden

Effect from foliage is even more important, in the exotic garden, than from flowers. The box elder, *Acer negundo*, has a variegated cultivar, 'Flamingo', in which the young growth includes a lot of pink and white. If you prune this pretty hard each winter, it will be stimulated into making new young growth through most of the summer,

instead of merely in one spring burst. You will at the same time be keeping it to a manageable size in a context where you don't want it to grow so large as to compete with fairly close neighbours. There is a canna, called 'Erebus', with glaucous leaves and salmon-pink flowers that looks handsome in front of the acer.

I have quite a scattering of yuccas, which are bold as evergreen plants and

Butterfly attractions

Escallonia bifida, a large shrub which needs protection, is the finest of all escallonias, being smothered, in late August and September, with panicles of starry white flowers. They are incredibly popular with butterflies. Another good butterfly plant is *Verbena bonariensis*, which grows to 1.8m/6ft and flowers and flowers for nearly four months. We can only allow a few of its myriad seedlings to develop, otherwise we should be engulfed. The plants are short-lived, two or three years being the limit, but they generally survive the winter with a 30cm/1ft or so of their growth intact, which makes the onset of flowering that much earlier.

In a hot, sunny bed that we keep on the dry side is a concentration of succulents, with a few cacti among them. We love cacti and would like to have lots of them. Of the succulents, aeoniums, both green- and purple-leaved, have stylish rosettes on a woody framework. The glaucous leaves of *Cotyledon orbiculata* are large and rounded, arranged in loose rosettes.

more than a little exciting when they carry their candelabrums of waxy, white bells. *Yucca gloriosa* is the largest of these. Then I have two kinds of New Zealand flax, tufted evergreens with strap leaves. One, *Phormium cookianum* subsp. *hookeri* 'Tricolor', is absolutely hardy here. It has rather lax, arching leaves, variegated in green, cream and purple. Flowering freely in early summer, it doubles its height to 1.8m/6ft,

and although the flowers themselves are smallish, tubular and of muted colouring, the aggregate of many flowering stems makes a strong and exotic impression. The other flax, 'Sundowner' (1.5m/5ft), is more of the upright *P. tenax* habit. There is a lot of pink in its leaf variegation and that looks good near to the pink *Canna* 'Louis Cayeux'. 'Sundowner' can look pretty unhappy at winter's end and may be in need of a good

deal of tidying up. But after a mild winter, it
sails through without blenching. In any case
it will have recovered by midsummer

This garden was originally a cattle
yard and Lutyens made his formal design
around a circular brick cattle drinking tank,
which stands about 90cm/3ft above the
surrounding paving. Like the other three,
elsewhere, I have filled it in with soil, and
we here grow the giant reed grass, *Arundo*

donax. It is hardy and rises to 3.6m/12ft or
so from nothing, with glaucous foliage. A
fine, rather bamboo-like central feature.
There is another at ground level in one
corner. These are thirsty plants.

Bananas add a truly exotic touch, having
such large leaves. These do tear into ribbons
in a high wind, but in this protected garden
they retain their integrity for many weeks.
The hardiest is a Japanese species, *Musa*

basjoo, and we leave that out all winter, but wrapped up in a jacket of fern fronds. In a real July heat wave, one new leaf will be produced every ten days – eight days is the record. To see them unfurling is an excitement in itself. When the main stem flowers, that is the end of it, but *M. basjoo* makes suckers, which we detach in spring.

In a shady bed, on the north side of a yew hedge, I grow shade-loving begonias, with notable success from *Begonia scharffii*. It has furry leaves tinged red on the underside, grows to nearly 90cm/3ft and flowers freely, with flesh-pink blossom. I also put my streptocarpus out, here. At the height of summer, when shadows are at their shortest, even this bed is sunny and the streptocarpus don't like that but they come into their own from August on. There are ferns, too, notably *Phlebodium aureum*, with deeply cut glaucous fronds, and *Cyrtomium falcatum*, with glossy, pinnate fronds.

The Egyptian papyrus, *Cyperus papyrus*, is a thrilling plant when it gets going, throwing up 2.4m/8ft, naked stems which are crowned by a mop of thread-fine leaves. We find this harder to overwinter than others in our collection, but manage to secure some of it one way or another, and seed germinates readily. Easier to manage is *Amicia zygomeris*, which is leguminous, with beautiful pinnate foliage that always attracts attention. At dusk, the leaves lose turgidity and collapse. Sizeable yellow pea flowers are produced at unexpected moments, but in no great quantity. We lift and house our stock, or propagate it from cuttings, which come on quickly, but if you plant amicia against a warm wall it can be treated as a permanency. After cutting the old stems down to the ground in spring, it will often make 1.8m/6ft or more of growth in one year.

Another notable foliage plant is *Furcraea parmentieri*. Superficially it resembles a yucca, but makes a huge crown of glaucous leaves that are not stiff or spine-tipped. When it flowers it dies, but leaves a host of tiny offspring by way of a legacy.

There is a short view through the centre of the exotic garden which I terminate at one end with a splendid foliage plant, *Colocasia esculenta*. This aroid, known in the US as elephant's ears, has fleshy, edible roots and is a feature in Chinese markets. But I grow it for its great shovel-shaped leaves, which are utterly smooth and most beautifully veined, a feature which can best be appreciated when low sunlight provides backlighting. Dew forms readily on the leaf surfaces, and they even start to drip from the sharp tip as early as 5 o'clock in the afternoon. Once they get going, there's a drip every three seconds or so.

Climbers and other woody highlights

A number of clematis will be performing but I really never know from year to year which of them will come out on top and which will suddenly let me down. *Clematis* 'Huldine' is a charmer, with slightly cupped, pearly white flowers only 10cm/4in or 12cm/5in across, and pale mauve on the underside. It is vigorous but also wayward, refusing to flower liberally in some positions. You may need to move it around to find out what suits it. 'Ville de Lyon' usually has a second go on its young wood – such a nice shape and I like the darker red of its sepal rims.

Sharing the wall behind is the evergreen self-clinging *Pileostegia viburnoides*. It is vigorous and has handsome leaves, but August is its flowering month when (not every year) it becomes smothered in a haze of tiny creamy white flowers. It is hardy and will thrive on any aspect but must be given a good start. The foot of a wall is often desperately dry. If this is so, plant it forward a bit, then feed and water it well until it has got away.

Of the annual climbers that we enjoy growing, *Thunbergia alata* has a rotate flower opening from a tube. Brightest, most contrasty and best is the orange-flowered kind, with a black centre. Fergus is extremely successful with *Rhodochiton atrosanguineus*, which he sows the previous autumn and

brings on under glass in individual pots. It flowers for ages and looks entirely original, with trails of purple flowers at every stage of their development and decay.

The garden's best single plant in this, its season, is *Hydrangea aspera* Villosa Group, but you must get the best form. Its lanceolate leaves are furry; the lacecap inflorescences have rich lilac sterile florets around the rim while the central fertile ones are pure blue and rich in pollen, which honey bees collect.

Right next to this and flowering at the same time is a tall column of *Eucryphia* × *nymansensis* 'Nymansay'. It never fails to be covered by white blossom, the numerous stamens having red tips. This is scented and rich in nectar, which the bees, especially the wild bees, forage for from dawn on.

To return to hydrangeas, the hardy *Hydrangea paniculata* cultivars, always

Hydrangea macrophylla 'Ayesha' – that of the polished, incurved, porcelain-like florets – flowers throughout August and has some effective companionship not far away with a pale yellow poker, Kniphofia 'Torchbearer' and teasels in flower.

white, flower this month on their young wood, with cone-shaped inflorescences. I best like those wherein sterile florets are sprinkled through a haze of fertile ones. A favourite, *H.p.* 'Kyushu', grows in the high garden with the pinky mauve, 1.2m/4ft, Japanese-type *Anemone tomentosa.*

Myrtus communis is right by the terrace door, so that its spicy fragrance is even better placed to waft through the house than the jasmine's. The other myrtle I grow is *Luma apiculata,* from Chile. This flowers in flushes – white but no scent. A hard winter will clobber mine, though it always recovers, and it self-sows freely.

Perhaps a contender for the award of best August-flowering shrub is *Itea ilicifolia.* It is evergreen with rather thin leaves of a crisp, papery texture, margined in mock prickles. The tiny flowers are borne in pendent, catkin-like racemes up to 30cm/1ft long, and they are green, heavily night (and early morning) scented of lemons. The ornamental bramble *Rubus cockburnianus* 'Goldenvale' is luminous with its lime-green foliage and now has poking out from its skirts the chains of blue trumpets from an old clump of willow gentian, *Gentiana asclepiadea.* Once you have the gentian in a place that it enjoys, it self-sows and I have quite a bit of it.

It is a full and busy month but never less than enjoyable.
A hint of autumn creeps in from time to time – one can be
sure of that, but it is no cause for lament. I love autumn.

Annuals

One of the best ways to make good the increasing shortfall, in August, of perennials in flower, is to grow plenty of annuals from seed and to make sure that they will be coming on when they are most needed, which will be from mid-month until October. Some, like annual asters, will do this naturally anyway. Others can be manipulated through date of sowing.

I (and Fergus too) am passionate about large-flowered zinnias – those with flat (not rolled-back) rays, called dahlia-flowered, double and in an amazing range of colours which you'd think would quarrel violently, but in fact they are immensely stimulating. The chief danger to zinnias is that chilly, wet weather will start up botrytis rot and it can spread quickly. But if you choose a sunny site, there'll be a good chance of success. These zinnias grow to 90cm/3ft but I like some of the smaller, bushy types too, notably *Zinnia* 'Chippendale', which is bronze with yellow tips to the rays. We scatter them among mixed plantings, for instance of *Crocosmia × crocosmiiflora* 'Solfaterre', which has apricot-orange flowers and bronze leaves.

Tithonia rotundifolia 'Torch' is like a zinnia, but grows to 1.5m/5ft at least. The large, hairy heart-leaves are crowned by single zinnia flowers in an amazingly pure, rich shade of orange. In the same mood category are marigolds, *Tagetes*.

It must be understood that I am writing of plants treated as annuals although, technically, they may be perennials.

Bright, untarnished green is precious in late summer, and you find it in the annual *Kochia* 'Evergreen', which makes a cone-shaped plant of rather formal outline and 90cm/3ft tall if grown well.

I like annuals that make big plants, even if they do require a stake and a tie. Thus, *Cosmos bipinnatus* 'Purity' at 1.5m/5ft has a lot more to offer in size of bloom and style of plant than the 60cm/2ft 'Sonata White'. A coloured strain that we hold in high regard is 'Dazzler' (1.2m/4ft), which opens intense carmine but fades gracefully to burgundy-red. We use that in all sorts of ways. With the purple foliage of *Ricinus communis* 'Carmencita', for instance.

If an annual can look like a shrub, it is doing well, because that means it has structure, which many annuals lack. Notable, then, is the spider flower, *Cleome pungens* (1.5m/5ft). It flowers for two or three months.

The colouring can be pink, white or bright mauve or a mixture, which is also compatible. I like this with *Ageratum houstonianum* 'Blue Horizon' (60cm/2ft) in front.

Tall annual rudbeckias are good. A successful combination was 'Indian Summer' (90cm/3ft), with its prominent black disc in the centre of powerfully yellow rays, with the lavender bedding verbena 'La France' in front and a permanent planting behind wherein white Japanese anemones and the white-variegated foliage of dogwood, *Cornus alba* 'Elegantissima', predominate.

Salvia coccinea 'Lady in Red' (60cm/2ft) has a nice habit but plenty of flower power. If the first crop is deadheaded, it usually succeeds in presenting a second. It contrasts well with another annual sage, the blue *S. farinacea* 'Victoria', which is naturally rather late flowering.

Dahlias

There is no flower, at this season, to touch the dahlia for contributing brilliant, clean colour over a long period. The flower shapes, whether single or double, cactus, water lily-like or so-called decorative, are beautiful, too. I go in for the medium- or small-flowered kinds which flower the most freely. Generally, the dahlia leaf is pretty uninteresting and needs to be kept in the background. The smaller-flowered kinds also have discreet foliage.

Dahlia 'David Howard' is my best friend, a neat, smallish decorative of cheerful, apricot-orange colouring and having darkish leaves. It flowers untiringly and eventually reaches a height of 1.8m/6ft. An excellent companion for this is the castor oil bean, *Ricinus communis* 'Carmencita', which has bold, bronze, palmate leaves and, as a bonus, a red inflorescence. Or, for contrast, I like the tall, white-flowered *Cosmos bipinnatus* 'Purity'. Coming down to a more reasonable level at the border's margin, a good mixer, grown from seed as a foliage plant, is *Grevillea robusta*, pinnate and bronze-tinted while young.

Because of its ferny purple foliage, the single (or semi-single) red 'Bishop of Llandaff' is a particular favourite even with those gardeners who disdain the majority of dahlias. That contrasts well with the blue foliage of *Eucalyptus gunnii*. Another

Dahlia 'David Howard' and *Canna* 'Wyoming' are among the great contributors to the general excitement of the exotic garden, as much for their leaves as for their bundles of silken flowers.

single I like is the pale yellow 'Clair de Lune', which also has a pale yellow collar of smaller rays.

Of the other red dahlias, the medium semi-cactus 'Witteman's Superba' is a special favourite with Fergus and myself; the hint of purple on the reverse side of its rays being especially subtle.

On the whole I have a preference for the warm shades – red, orange and bronze – but I do like the clear pink, water lily-style (with an open-textured arrangement of rounded petals) 'Pearl of Heemstede', and this plays its part in an overall pink gathering with *Salvia involucrata* 'Bethellii' (1.5m/5ft), which is quite a vicious shade of pink with mauve thrown in; the self-sowing, mauve-pink *Impatiens balfourii* (90cm/3ft); and the beautiful cherry-pink *Canna iridiflora*, with very large, purple-rimmed green leaves and a gracefully arching inflorescence.

Perennials in season

There has to be a certain falling off in flower power from many perennials, after the middle of the month. From the border phloxes, for instance, but some of these, like *Phlox paniculata* 'Duchess of York', in two shades of pink, flower late, while others give us a second flowering, more generous in some years than in others. There are also, if you look for them, plenty of perennials that actually come on in August. In the long border, for instance, *Buddleja* 'Lochinch' now covers its grey-green foliage with long spikes of lavender flowers. I have three patches of *Artemisia lactiflora* in the long border and two elsewhere in the garden, so valuable a plant do I consider this to be.

I have *Hydrangea macrophylla* 'Mariesii', here, a semi-lacecap, with flat heads of (with me) pink flowers having a scattering of large, sterile florets in the centre of the disc as well as around the margins. Another valued shrub is the summer-flowering tamarisk, *Tamarix ramosissima*, with plumes of pink spikelets set among feathery foliage. Leaning over the back of this are the 2.4m/8ft cardoons, which flower all this month. They have rich lavender-blue discs (covered in bees), which always look a muddier shade of mauve in photos.

At the front of this piece of border is an excellent mixer, the popular polyantha rose 'The Fairy'. A really clear, clean shade of

Early in the month, I cut the whole group of Alchemilla mollis *hard back to the ground and it soon refurnishes with a new crop of young leaves.*

pink, set among glossy foliage. That mixes with self-sown Chinese chives, *Allium tuberosum*, 60cm/2ft tall with umbels of white flowers, the inflorescence retaining its shape all through the winter.

Lower down the border, *Aster sedifolius* (*A. acris*) comes into its own with a duvet of interlocking mauve daisies. At 90cm/3ft, it needs and deserves the best support with pea sticks. If I can get a self-sown, scarlet nasturtium to thread through this patch and flower with it, that is ideal.

In the high garden, there is a large area of stock bed which we have planted with a view to its looking nice as well as being useful. A theme of self-sown purple orach, *Atriplex hortensis*, runs through it but will have to be pulled out at the end of the month before it sheds its seeds incontinently. It does combine extraordinarily well with many perennials, for instance the sunflower, now

coming on, *Helianthus* 'Capenoch Star' (1.5m/5ft), bright yellow with an anemone-centred disc. Also with *Phlox paniculata* var. *alba*.

Again with atriplex nearby, there is a patch of crocosmia which I have called 'Late Lucifer', it being a seedling of 'Lucifer' which usefully flowers a couple of weeks later. A good contrast can be made with that (or with 'Lucifer' itself), and *Aconitum* 'Spark's Variety' (1.2m/4ft). This is deep blue but has the advantage that its laterals are as vigorous and important as the central spike. All appear to flower together.

As you come up the steps from the orchard garden, the angle of the path turns; you are between short, double hedges covered with the red blossom of *Fuchsia* 'Riccartonii', but immediately beyond I have loudly contrasting patches of a bright purple phlox, behind, and bright

Above: A late-flowering stock bed in the high garden glows in the late summer light.

Below: The central feature of *Kniphofia* 'Nobilis' continues to dominate the long border, with its brilliant orange pokers, all through the month. I would emphasize how important it is, with these pokers, to keep up with the task of removing faded spikes so that they do not mar the continuing display made by those that are later-flowering.

Top: One more combination of perennials that you might not have thought of! A pink Japanese anemone – any pink one – with the pale yellow sunflower, *Helianthus* 'Lemon Queen' (1.8m/6ft or more). This has quite small daisies and it gradually builds up a display which reaches its peak next month.

Above: The top of the long border at its peak is here filled with abundant phloxes.

yellow *Leontodon ringens*, in front. This is a composite with clustered yellow daisies above broad, undivided leaves. Nearby, and tastefully toning the loud company down, is the silver-variegated form of *Calamagrostis* × *acutiflora*, called 'Overdam' (1.5m/5ft); an upright feature that contributes helpfully for more than half the year.

Another supportive grass now and for many months to come is *Stipa splendens* (90cm/3ft), with arching plumes that are feathery on first flowering, but close up and become pale beige in colouring. It is an excellent landscape feature. In the barn garden, I have it in front of *Miscanthus floridulus*, which has a fountain-like habit, rising within a few months to 3.6m/12ft and having an entirely foliar role.

Yet another superb yellow daisy will now be at its best, *Rudbeckia laciniata* 'Herbstsonne' (2m/7ft).

Other jobs for the month

Sowing

- Sow sweet scabious, or pin-cushion flower, *Scabiosa atropurpurea* (90cm/3ft), to flower from July on next year.
- Make late sowings of annual poppies.

Dealing with the produce

- Regularly harvest the abundance of vegetables, including artichokes and lettuces.
- Crop tomatoes grown outside, such as 'Sungold'.
- Pick autumn-fruiting raspberries by the end of the month.

Routine care

- Protect ripening crops of cherries, apricots, peaches and figs against birds.
- Start to cut long grass areas such as meadows.

I think 'Autumn Bliss' raspberries have as good a flavour as any variety I know. The yellow 'Fallgold' is very sweet (honey bees will besiege it in a droughty spell) but not strong on flavour.

Poppy companions

Among our favourites is the so-called tulip poppy, *Hunnemannia fumariifolia*, which is something between a poppy and an eschscholzia, with purest yellow poppy flowers set off by deeply cut, glaucous foliage. They contrast particularly well with bright purple-flowered *Verbena rigida* (45cm/1½ft). Another good companion would be an apron of the prostrate, blue-flowered pimpernel, *Anagallis monellii* subsp. *linifolia*. A really intense blue and often mistaken for a gentian. I always grow some of that.

September

The early autumn garden, here, is full of
energy and ideas, reflecting our love of the
season. The light is no longer so hard in the
middle of the day, so the plants look happier.
The gathering swallows twitter in the skies
and the house martins, which used to sun
themselves in huge quantities on the long
roof of our barn and on the great hall roof,
are now performing the last of their mad, glad
whirlings and acrobatics, often over the horse
pond. However, there's little point in nostalgia
when the present is also good in its way.

Crocuses and colchicums

There is a fairly urgent time factor on cutting some of the meadow areas, before their little season of flowers from colchicums and autumn crocuses gets going. We usually give it a second cut before the first cuts elsewhere have been completed. This ensures a nice low background for *Crocus nudiflorus* when that gets going. Exactly when it gets going depends very much on how dry the ground is. A heavy shower, and away it goes, but drought will hold it back for several weeks. Mid-month would be average in a moist year. This crocus is a rich purple with yellow stamens, and it stands upright on a strongish stem. It spreads by a stoloniferous habit, so that a single corm will make quite a patch, in time. I was interested to see, at Belsay Hall in Northumberland, where this crocus is colonized as at Dixter, that it flowers several weeks earlier, simply because conditions are so much moister. The fact that they are a lot further north, and therefore cooler, makes no difference.

The other autumn-flowering crocus that naturalizes well in turf is *C. speciosus*. We have a lot of that in various places, and the flowering time of these colonies depends on their location. *Crocus speciosus* has a long, weak stalk and is apt to lie on its elbow, after the first day. I don't find that objectionable. It gives the bluest impression of any crocus, by dint of its heavy veining. The stigmas

(or stigmata) are brilliant scarlet and the flowers, if you get down to their level, are deliciously scented. Where you have a big colony of *C. speciosus*, it is noticeable that the spring-flowering crocuses cannot compete.

I have colchicums in the meadows; they stay alive but hardly increase. The pink in their colouring readily distinguishes them from any crocus. My best colonies are in the borders. One of the most prosperous-looking, with substantial, waxy white cups, is the late-September flowering *Colchicum speciosum* 'Album', and my mat-forming background for that is *Helichrysum petiolare* 'Variegatum', which is less vigorous and so less competitive than straight *H. petiolare*. Another good place for a vigorous colchicum is interplanted with *Alchemilla mollis*. From having been cut back six weeks earlier, that is now covered with fresh foliage, which gives the colchicum just the background that suits it.

Bulbs

Some autumn-flowering bulbs or corms give you a feeling, if not actually of spring, at least of the year's renewable cycle. The hardy *Cyclamen hederifolium* is like that. Its tubers increase in size from year to year, indefinitely. They rest in summer, then carry their galaxies of pinky mauve or white flowers from late July into November.

Nerine bowdenii is a splendid autumn performer (see below). It is as vivid a pink (with a dash of mauve) as you could imagine and an entirely un-autumnal colour, but no less welcome for that. It is a tremendously willing and prolific flowerer, even in shade. Its leaves, in a hot climate, would die away in summer. In ours, they often survive into the flowering period and look rather awful, so I believe in removing them in late August, before flowering stems have shown themselves.

Where are the songs of spring!
Aye, where are they?
Think not of them, thou hast thy music too.

Keats, 'Ode to Autumn'

Grouping plants

In the barn garden, facing north-west and at the back of quite a deep border, I'm really pleased with a combination that starts off with the 1.8m/6ft *Aconitum carmichaelii* Wilsonii Group 'Kelmscott', which has deep blue monkshoods; and that is next to the white racemes of *Actaea simplex* (1.8m/6ft), in a purple-leaved form, though the colouring of the leaves counts for little by the end of the season. Beyond these, a favourite annual – the 2m/7ft *Polygonum orientale*, with great sprays of short, deep pink racemes. It is absolutely at its best in September. Near to this trio, I have had the rich yellow, black-eyed daisies of *Rudbeckia hirta* 'Indian Summer' (1.2m/4ft), which flowers for more than two months from mid-August. A splendid annual. I also like to use the polygonum at the top of the long border, behind my strongest group of single white Japanese anemones, right next to Lutyens's oak seat. That, as a full-stop, has the rosettes of spiky, grey-green leaves of *Astelia chathamica*, at its orchard end. The astelia shows up from the other end of the border and I only hope that a cold winter won't kill it.

On a more intimate scale and with a good deal of shade, *Arum italicum* subsp. *italicum* 'Marmoratum', which is currently without foliage, has a crop of scarlet berries, gathered into a club-like knob. Also small-

Opposite: The scarlet berries of *Arum italicum* subsp. *italicum* 'Marmoratum' go well with bright green polypody ferns and with the dwarf hardy *Fuchsia* 'Tom Thumb'.

Below: I find a most satisfactory grouping is of *Rudbeckia hirta* 'Indian Summer', *Aconitum carmichaelii* Wilsonii Group 'Kelmscott', *Actaea simplex* Atropurpurea Group and *Persicaria orientalis*.

scale but this time in the sun, the magenta *Geranium* × *riversleaianum* 'Russell Prichard', which has been flowering since May, is still threaded through grey *Artemisia ludoviciana* 'Silver Queen', but is joined by the stiff, purple-headed *Verbena rigida*. This verbena is not much more than 30cm/1ft tall, whereas our old friend *V. bonariensis* is 1.8m/6ft and that now has for company *Patrinia scabiosifolia* (1.5m/5ft), whose

inflorescence of heads of tiny flowers is very like the verbena's but clear yellow with a touch of green.

In the stock bed, the plantings are mainly for late summer and autumn. Behind *Plectranthus argentatus* (60cm/2ft) and increasingly abundant throughout the month is the mildew-resistant Michaelmas daisy *Aster* 'Little Carlow', lavender verging on blue. We keep it down to 90cm/3ft

by frequent replanting. Next to it, the abundantly flowering black-eyed-susan, *Rudbeckia fulgida* var. *deamii*, which is the most cheerful yellow imaginable. There's the white, papery-textured *Anaphalis margaritacea* var. *yedoensis* (90cm/3ft) which is more stylish than others in this genus because of its height. In the background, there is the solidity of shrubs, notably the hard-pruned golden catalpa, *Catalpa*

Opposite: Good foliage comes into its own in a shady corner adorned with *Clerodendrum bungei*, × *Fatshedera lizei* and *Hedera colchica* 'Dentata Variegata'.

Below: I have a good patch of *Plectranthus argentatus*, for its large, rounded, silver-grey foliage, as well as *Anaphalis margaritacea* var. *yedoensis*, *Aster* 'Little Carlow', *Rudbeckia fulgida* var. *deamii* and *Miscanthus sinensis* 'Strictus' in this late-flowering stock bed.

bignonioides 'Aurea'.

As the month progresses, the pampas grasses rouse themselves from their slumbers and I have the 1.8m/6ft 'dwarf' *Cortaderia selloana* 'Pumila', with silken, upright white plumes, highlighting the scarlet hips of sweet briar, *Rosa rubiginosa*. This was accidental in the first place but then became intentional. Two other roses contribute with their hips, now, in a mixed border setting. In *R. setipoda* they are long and hairy, borne more or less singly. But in *R. glauca* they are in clusters; not a sharp red – quite subdued, really, but they show up well enough. This famous rose has purplish glaucous leaves and goes well with pink Japanese anemones – 'Hadspen Abundance' in this case – and the orangey fruit looks just as good with the anemone.

Ampelopsis brevipedunculata 'Elegans'

It is always fun to think of ways in which to group your plants rather than to treat them as solo items, although that often happens too.

has such variegated leaves that there is little for it to fall back on in the way of green. The variegation is pink and white and its stems and tendrils are pink. We find that the best way to grow it is on the flat and we feed it heavily. That goes well with the very similar pink of a bedding verbena called 'Silver Anne', whose rambling habit encourages it to investigate its neighbours. A trio is made up with the shrubby *Ceratostigma*

willmottianum, which is a relatively hardy plumbago with deep blue flowers; real blue, not mauvy. If this can bring its old growth through the previous winter intact, it will start flowering in July, but if it has to start again from ground level, it will only now be getting into its stride and its flowering period will be curtailed at the other end by cold nights. By and large, I get value from my plant, even though it does not have the wall protection that would enable it to grow much larger and more strongly.

In a house-shaded but protected corner of the wall garden, where the sun scarcely penetrates, the suckering shrub *Clerodendrum bungei* is blooming freely throughout the month, with upright, terminal domes of scented pink blossom above darkest green heart-leaves. I love this plant, although it does sucker incontinently. This has more good foliage around it, notably of × *Fatshedera lizei*, a hybrid between fatsia and hedera, with large, glossy, bright green leaves.

Further along the border and still pretty shaded, I have a colony of the hardy *Begonia grandis* subsp. *evansiana* (38cm/15in), which flowers in autumn but only if the weather suits it (I cannot make out exactly which weather that is). That has a pink Japanese anemone behind it and the second flowering of white *Hydrangea macrophylla* 'Madame

The best of Dixter in September

Solo performers

Some plants display themselves most fully if they don't have competition from close neighbours, while others lack companions because I have not yet worked out what these could appropriately be. My most glamorous hedychium, 'Tara', has a corner to itself and has to be a feast in itself, which is not difficult. The foliage is handsome, as in the whole genus, but the terminal racemes of orange flowers are arrestingly showy. Each flowering spike is fairly short-lived, so perhaps this is a comet rather than a star.

Allium senescens subsp. *montanum*, which was also flowering through most of August, makes a low mat of grey-green foliage with a twist on it, so that the leaves are arranged in swirls. Then a mass of flowering globes, rather like thrift, *Armeria*, and a nice shade of mauve. These are extremely popular with bees and butterflies.

Another performer attractive to insects, because of its mass of sickly-sweet-smelling globes of green flowers, is the bush ivy, *Hedera helix* f. *poetarum* 'Poetica Arborea'. Its foliage is dark and lustrous and it is an excellent solo performer, although I have put it with a suitable neighbour right behind it – the golden catalpa, whose height I keep down to 2m/7ft by winter pruning.

The South American *Eryngium pandanifolium* is a noble evergreen perennial.

It has long, narrow, saw-edged leaves, a bit on the glaucous side. The splendidly branching flower candelabrums rise to 2m/7ft or more in autumn, and each branchlet terminates in a little globe of discreetly dove-coloured florets. I spotted a version of it growing in the Chelsea Physic Garden, in which the flower heads are rich purple and stand forth boldly. I was given a piece of this and it is even more telling than the original. Such plants are so unusual in appearance that their star quality stands forth plainly for all to see.

In its way, the hawthorn *Crataegus orientalis* is another such. In shape, it develops quite a presence. The deeply cut leaves are grey, throughout the season. Clusters of white flowers open in June and are followed, in the second half of September, by a glamorous crop of large haws, luminously coloured soft orange (not red). This grows by the front path and is possibly the most noticed plant in my garden.

A more mundane but still handsome hawthorn, by the front path and also in the orchard, is *C. persimilis* 'Prunifolia'. Like all the American thorns, its leaves are oval and undivided. Its white flowers come a few days later than our British thorns' and the heavy crops of fruit, ripening late September and sometimes carried well after leaf-fall, are very dark red – so dark that they need sunshine to warm them up. If this hawthorn is cropping only lightly, its foliage will take on splendid fall tints, but if great effort has been expended in fruit production the leaves drop without colouring much. It frequently self-sows in my garden, with the help of birds.

Another conventional touch of autumn is provided by a spindle given me by Beth Chatto. It looks like a form of our native

A foggy autumn morning in the exotic garden.

Dahlia 'Witteman's Superba' dominates the foreground in this September scene of the exotic garden.

Euonymus europaeus, but it is an abundant and, so far as I can tell, regular fruiter. (Spindles can be disappointing in this respect.) The fruit is borne on older wood, not on the young shoots. It is bright pink until the aril, enclosing the seeds, splits, and they are orange. It is one of nature's daring combinations but, of course, it comes off. They always do. One of the many flowering grasses next to this is in pleasing contrast.

The exotic garden

This is a major feature all through September, though there is little more to be said about it that I didn't say last month. Everything, of course, gets larger and there is more deadheading to keep up with. The dahlias are sure to be good. The cannas' foliage can be depended upon but their flowers may rot prematurely if the weather is unkind. The streptocarpus improve and the begonias approve of not being beaten upon by too hot a sun. *Cotyledon orbiculata* becomes outrageously lush and there are some enormous rosettes on *Aeonium arboreum*, which looks as though it is receiving signals from outer space. Surprisingly (to me) it sometimes wilts in sun.

Other jobs for the month

Sowing

O Early in September, make salad sowings that have a good chance of surviving the winter.

O Sow rocket, *Eruca vesicaria* subsp. *sativa*; with luck, you can be picking it from next month till April.

Dealing with produce

O Cut the first 'Romanesco' broccoli heads as they mature.

O Harvest vegetables such as gourds, cucumbers and beans.

O Continue to pick raspberries regularly.

O Pick 'Williams' pears, if the tree is fruiting this year; fruit will be ripe within ten days of harvesting – a strong, sweet, musky flavour that I love.

Routine care

O Check sprouts and purple-sprouting broccoli for cabbage white caterpillars; control as appropriate.

O Keep going through the borders tidying up.

O Finish off cutting the long grass areas.

Yew hedges

The shaggy yew hedges are being assiduously trimmed throughout September. We start with the eighteen peacocks, so that they shall look smart at the time when the double hedges of *Aster lateriflorus* var. *horizontalis* are building up their flower power. Then we move to the long border and the stretch of hedge running at right angles from that down the side of the orchard. Next, across the orchard to the exotic garden, but here we trim only their outside and top; the inside is left till we have cleared the beds in front of them. And finally, on across to the topiary garden.

October

The sharp smell of October is most attractive and is largely created, I imagine, by drifts of fallen leaves. I never tire of scuffling through them. Unless the leaves are seriously shading plants that need to see the light, we are in no hurry to pick them up and take them, as we eventually do, to spread around rhododendrons as a moisture-retaining mulch. We wait for the wind to blow them into sheltered corners, from where they will the more easily be gathered. Principal leaf-fall starts in the last week and the ash trees are among the earliest to shed. Their leaf stalks make a companionable tapping as they hit the tiles of the potting shed roof.

Asters

There are lots of lovely asters of the Michaelmas daisy type, though I do limit myself fairly strictly to those that remain healthy without our help and to those that do not present a dull and solid block of boring foliage all through the summer. The double hedges of *Aster lateriflorus* var. *horizontalis* that link the topiary peacocks have been building up since their first daisies appeared in early September. They reach their climax on 17 October (I promise) and need no excuse to be visited every few hours – they are in any case conveniently on my way to herbs, salads and green vegetables for last-minute picking. Their leaves (scarcely visible by now) are purplish and the prominent daisy discs are purple, while the rays, which are slightly reflexed, are white, though tinted.

I have an amazing little aster from Beth Chatto, *A. ericoides* f. *prostratus* 'Snow Flurry'. Its tight little branches hug the ground and now, for a couple of weeks, carry dense white, undulating drifts of tiny, pure white daisies. It is on the edge of the square in the centre of the high garden and I interrupt its flow with the upright spears of bronze evergreen *Libertia peregrinans*. Also supposedly an *Aster ericoides* hybrid is the 60cm/2ft cultivar called 'Esther'. Although not flowering till September–October, 'Esther' has exceptionally bright green foliage, small and neat, so it is not a

Opposite: The habit of *Aster lateriflorus* var. *horizontalis* is by no means solid, but stylishly spreading, with branch tips taking off and doing their own thing. Very firm of texture, however.

Below: In front of *Aster lateriflorus* var. *horizontalis* I grow low bands of the prostrate, neat-leaved *Persicaria vacciniifolia*. It is a perfect foil to the asters, having, at the same season, stiffly upright pokers of tiny pink flowers.

complete passenger in the summer border. Meanwhile *A. pilosus* var. *pringlei* 'Monte Cassino' scarcely merits border space throughout the summer. Raised from spring cuttings, it's grown on in pots, so it is easy to fill a gap with it at the last moment, in early October, if we're being extremely keen. It is naturally at its best in the last half of the month, pure white, only 75cm/2½ft tall on young plants and with leaves that remain fresh. This is popular in the cut flower market and its season of flowering can be manipulated, as with chrysanthemums.

Of the tall Michaelmas daisies, I like to have a few plants of old 'Climax', which makes a widely branching pyramid and carries single, lavender-mauve daisies. *Aster turbinellus* (1.5m/5ft) is a winner, with fine, intricately branching growth, all purple-tinted, and spangled purple daisies.

The best of Dixter in October

Some of the great later flowerers

The smell of chrysanthemum foliage and, to a lesser extent, flowers, is entirely individual, richly autumnal and with a satisfying sharpness. I do not grow any chrysanthemum seriously – they are a little demanding or, if not demanding, a little bit boring. But I love to have them around me. Sometimes, if we have grown a good batch in a row, we move them into the borders just as the first flowers are coming out and are showing us what their colour is. Most of what we have are grown from seed – the F1 'Fanfare' strain – which are mixed. So, come the autumn, we can pick out those we should like to see again. The double, brownish kinds are often the earliest flowering, which is useful for border display. But the later ones, right into November if frosts hold off, are so good to pick, though you'll need to strip most of their foliage and give them a deep drink, if they are to last in water.

Meanwhile the sunflowers keep going and the yellow quality in the light suits their colouring to perfection. If you believe that the best is good enough for you, then *Helianthus* 'Monarch' will be hard to beat. It is a large, black-eyed daisy, superb against a blue sky, and is easily arranged as its own height is around 2.4m/8ft. I am apt to pinch out some (only a small proportion) of the side-shoots, so that the terminal bloom is – I was going to say outsize, but that sounds vulgar. What I do is to leave all the side-shoots on some stems and remove them all from the selected few. In this way, you achieve the ideal of many blooms of varying size.

Although of secondary importance to its foliar contributions, *Helianthus salicifolius* flowers at last. The terminal 90cm/3ft of a 2.7m/9ft stem branches out and carries quite small but charming black-eyed daisies. You may get them at 2.7m/9ft, and see them against the sky (always blue, of course), or the stem may have been blown sideways at some stage, which doesn't really matter, as the top rights itself to the vertical within hours, but the flowers will then be seen low down and quite a distance from where the plant was sited. In one unpremeditated case I enjoyed them among the rich carmine and red of *Cosmos bipinnatus* 'Dazzler'.

The late-flowering *Salvia uliginosa* (1.8m/6ft) is abundant, at last, with short spikes of light, but pure, blue flowers, each with a white fleck at its centre. That goes with any colour – pale yellow, pink, red – but is a wasted catalyst if segregated altogether. As it is a see-through plant, I often grow it near the border's margin.

Hesperantha coccinea (45cm/1½ft) is a real autumn flower, but it is hard to predict when its season will start. Early September is

Fuchsia magellanica 'Versicolor', which tends to look tired and dusty in high summer, has taken on a new lease of life with fresh young rosy-purple-tinted shoots and dripping clusters of its slender, blood-red flowers. Here it is growing alongside *Atriplex hortensis* var. *rubra* and *Stipa splendens*.

ideal, because it then runs on for a couple of months. But it may be a lot later. Sometimes it seems as though clumps that were newly divided in the spring are more precocious than old colonies; at others, not. The spikes of bowl-shaped flowers above iris-like leaves obviously relate it to gladioli and crocosmias. Even though it is an invasive plant, I have some half-dozen named cultivars. By far the most effective is *H. coccinea* 'Major',

which is strong red and quite large-flowered. Schizostylis love moisture (they will even thrive in shallow water) so my heavy soil suits them.

An autumn-flowerer of which I never have enough is *Saxifraga fortunei* (30cm/ 1ft). They make a great thing of it in Japan, where it is seen as a pot plant, and there are pink-flowered cultivars as well as the normal white. A deciduous perennial, it

I like *Kniphofia rooperi* in the barn garden with the 'dwarf' white pampas *Cortaderia selloana* 'Pumila', though that continues for a long time after the poker has been forgotten. The latter also looks good in front of *Melianthus major*, while self-sown teasels, albeit dark brown by now, are another strongly designed companion.

has scalloped leaves that are a feature in themselves; then a cloud of white, lopsided flowers, on which the two lowest petals are long and hang down like whiskers. It is happy in cool shade, and I combine it with a prolific autumn-flowering crocus, *Crocus pulchellus* – a clear, light shade of bluey mauve.

The coarsely glamorous *Impatiens tinctoria* (1.2m/4ft) only starts flowering seriously in October, although it should get going in June. Capsid damage to its growing shoots is mainly responsible. The leaves are really ugly, but its flowers, in white and purple, are amazing, and it seems right that they should be heavily night-scented in a slightly excessive and immoral way. The first touch of frost and it is gone, but the tuberous roots can be treated like a dahlia's, and they sometimes survive outside.

The dahlias that we had struck from late spring cuttings and subsequently used to replace early summer displays are now fresh and full of young vigour.

I have always preached that kniphofias should, to earn their space, have quite a long-flowering season with a succession of flowering spikes. I break this rule with *Kniphofia linearifolia* (1.5m/5ft), which is green all summer, but an unusually bright shade of green. Its flowering stems all rush up together in the first two weeks of October and they flower a good shade of orange, lasting no longer than two weeks. *Kniphofia rooperi* is also late, though with a slightly more spread-out season.

When on form, the climbing *Solanum laxum* 'Album' against the barn is one of my garden's most striking features through most of the second half of the year. It is generous with its open panicles of pure white flowers and yellow stamens. Once up to the barn's gutter, at 4.5m/15ft, it will continue on to the tiled roof and I can let it do that for a season without any damage.

Some October flowers are in continuation or a repeat of an earlier performance. Many of the cranesbills, for instance, like *Geranium endressii* and G. *sanguineum*, will come again with fresh foliage and a new crop of flowers if shorn back after their first flush. They may still be flowering, at that time, but have an out-at-elbows look which can be entirely redressed by firm action.

Hardy fuchsias are never so good as when it has become a little cool but not yet frosty. 'Mrs Popple' (90cm/3ft) is in a semi-sulk all summer – partly through capsid damage to its young shoots but I think there's more to it than that. Anyway, its heavy foliage is at last redeemed by a huge late crop of red and purple blossom. 'Genii' (60cm/2ft) is red and purple too, but with the added highlights of yellow-green foliage and red stalks and leaf veins. 'Enfant Prodigue' (90cm/3ft) goes through long barren periods, but that is suddenly a mass of red and purple blossom set among neat little leaves.

In the barn garden, dahlias make a contrast between ornamental grasses – miscanthus and cortaderia in flower and calamagrostis with bleached, upright stems. A combination that has pleased us is orange *Dahlia* 'Chiltern Amber' and the quite dwarf 'Ellen Huston'.

Annuals and bulbs

There is one obliging annual that I really must bring in; it is such a stayer. This is *Cuphea miniata* 'Firefly' (38cm/15in) (see below). It makes a little bush and we plant it out where there are alliums – *Allium neapolitanum*, all of whose growth we remove in June before it can seed, and *A. cristophii*, whose dying skeletons we leave and plant around. The cuphea has quite deep mauvy pink flowers on a neat bush and it continues without becoming tired or untidy until the frosts arrive.

Two more autumn-flowering bulbs must be mentioned. The flower of the west wind, *Zephranthes candida* (15cm/6in), has rush-like evergreen leaves; its flowers are like white crocuses. The flowers of *Sternbergia lutea* (12cm/5in) are superficially crocus-like too and a brilliant chrome yellow. It puts out fresh, dark green strap leaves.

I always hope that there will be worthwhile crops of mushrooms in our meadows. Now that these have been mown, the mushroom caps gleam from a distance. The best chance of a crop is when rains follow drought, but it needs to stay mild, too. Often, rain is followed by cold weather.

Grasses and bamboos

Many grasses are in perfect shape, now, and it always amazes me how many of them choose to flower in autumn. Although my garden is largish, it is divided into compartments and I think that most of these grasses show up best as solo features rather than in groups. They have quite sufficient structure and presence to deserve to stand well above the surrounding plants. This may often be achieved by siting them on a promontory or in a corner, but fairly near to a border's margin.

Two of my most effective ornamental grasses are 'Windspiel' and 'Transparent', both of which come under *Molinia caerulea* subsp. *arundinacea*. As the name of one of them indicates, they are see-through plants. 'Transparent' starts to look interesting as early as June. Only its basal tuft of foliage is a bit of a let-down; I should really have something lowish in front of it. But I warn that these important-looking grasses do dislike disturbance and will sulk for a full year after being split or moved (which must always be done in spring).

I often think I grow a lot of different bamboos, but if a bamboo nut visits I am soon disillusioned. I have scarcely started. Much as I love bamboos, they cannot just be chucked around. In a mixed border, you need to be careful about their habit, which may be either invasive or given to flopping over the neighbours. A floppy bamboo can look fine in a landscape setting, but there is a limit to my landscape settings. I keep looking for more of them.

I love the elegant *Himalayacalamus falconeri*, now at its best with slender wands that arch over and look wonderful, at the horizontal, when hung with translucent raindrops. But anywhere nearer than 2.4m/8ft to a path, and you'll be in for an involuntary shower-bath on frequent occasions. Some redress can be achieved with stake and string. In winter, this bamboo looks threadbare, but in spring the best treatment is to cut out every cane that is more than one season old. The last season's canes will still be without leaves, but they are smooth and olive-green and, without the weight of foliage, they stand up and look beautiful in a quite unexpected way, when the pruning has been completed.

Other jobs for the month

Sowing and other propagating
- Start off annuals so they are at their best in May.
- Take soft cuttings of bedding plants like verbenas and gazanias.

Dealing with produce
- Crop saladings and vegetables such as bulbous fennel.
- Lift maincrop 'Pink Fir Apple' potatoes, preferably in dry weather so that the tubers can be stored (in a bin, made for the purpose) with little mud attached.
- Pick and store late-season apples such as 'High Canons', a fairly small, light yellow cooker; it keeps till March.
- Gather any 'Doyenné du Comice' pears (see opposite), and wrap each pear in a plastic lettuce bag (with air vents in it); shrivelling is thereby prevented.
- Continue to pick autumn raspberries, until gales blow all the berries off.

Routine care
- Ensure that all tender succulents, the evergreen begonias varieties and streptocarpus have glass protection.

Annuals for sowing now
The five-spot, *Nemophila maculata*, which has purple spots at the tips of its off-white petals, is not too good at roughing it outside through the winter, so we raise that under glass, pot the seedlings individually and plant them out in March. It is the same story with *Omphalodes linifolia*, which is like a refined, grey-leaved gypsophila. Then cornflowers: we sow the blue *Centaurea cyanus* 'Jubilee' strain in early October and bring them on, some in large pots, to stand outside the porch, others in 10cm/4in squares, to plant in the borders in March and they'll flower on till July. *Cerinthe major* 'Purpurascens' is treated like this too. We also sow annual silene in autumn.

November

The month of November, in my part of the world, is widely reviled. The clocks have gone back, the days are rapidly shortening, it rains (wettest month of the year), it blows or else it settles down into gloomy fogs. Why is it that people so often remember only the weather's worst features? The brighter days are totally ignored and forgotten. November can be a month of largely beautiful weather. I remember the one when we were having our huge barn roof retiled. I took photographs of work in progress and they were invariably backed by blue skies. There wasn't a hitch. Good weather in November is not as rare as you think. Start making daily notes on it and you will see that I am right.

Autumn colour

Oaks take on their russet hues well into the month, while field maples turn bright yellow. When my thoughts are unfocused, I have often mistaken such a maple for a flowering broom. I grow two Japanese maples and they seem to like me well enough. *Acer palmatum* 'Sango-kaku' is the freshest imaginable green in spring. It now changes to clear yellow and then, as its leaves fall, reveals the pink colouring of its young twigs. Meanwhile the jagged leaves of compact and upright *A.p.* 'Shishigashira' are crimped, almost parsley-like and dark green, but they colour up quite late in autumn

Our mulberry turns yellow. Its leaf-fall can be a tame affair, spread over quite a period, but, if a frosty night occurs at the right moment, all its leaves fall within half an hour the next morning, lying as a thick carpet underneath the tree. Similarly the medlar never fails. Such a prettily shaped small tree, for a start; its foliage turns warm brown while its fruits, although themselves quite a dark brown, are fascinatingly shaped.

I have the hermaphrodite form of *Celastrus orbiculatus*, a deciduous climber whose leaves turn luminous yellow. When fallen, they reveal garlands of ochre-yellow, spherical fruit, which then split, themselves, to reveal scarlet seeds. Pick them quickly at this stage, before the weather spoils them. They make admirable winter decoration.

Oaks overhang the lower moat and on quiet days you hear the plop of their ripe acorns as they drop into the water.

Another hermaphrodite in my garden is a self-pollinating butcher's broom, *Ruscus aculeatus*, which is quite a low, mildly suckering evergreen shrub with dark green, sharply pointed foliage. Its large, crimson berries are freely borne in most years. They look amazing when struck by winter sunshine and last through to late spring the next year.

A surprising number of other evergreens also change colour in autumn. My most conspicuous example is the softly textured *Chamaecyparis thyoides* 'Ericoides'.

Ilex × *altaclerensis* 'Golden King', a virtually prickle-free holly with foliage broadly margined in yellow, makes a column at the top of the long border. It is a great feature at every season, but even more so than usual now that it has ripened its red berries. For, despite its masculine name, this is a female clone. Birds usually set about

it just before I want to pick some for the Christmas pudding, although in another year the berries will remain into spring.

There are self-sown *Cotoneaster horizontalis* all through the garden. This shrub has a wonderful structure, stiff, yet full of curves. There is usually a plentiful crop of its crimson-red berries and, if the birds have spared these, they contrast with the near magenta colouring that the foliage takes on late in the month.

A predominantly autumn-flowering shrub is the endearing, if insignificant, *Buddleja auriculata*, with panicles of tiny, buff-white flowers wafting as generously as did *B. davidii* in summer. *Buddleja auriculata* is evergreen and its foliage has none of the generally accepted buddleja coarseness. It will grow to 3.6m/12ft on a warm wall and does require wall protection. Its habit is mildly suckering; even if a harsh winter cuts it to the ground, it will return from suckers, once truly established.

At this season a grouping that I particularly enjoy is on the lower terrace. There is the oak-leaved *Hydrangea quercifolia*, whose purplish autumn colouring takes ages to mature. On its left and behind, a great rounded bush ivy, the adult manifestation of variegated *Hedera algeriensis* 'Gloire de Marengo'. It flowers very late and is now smothered in globular umbels of ivy blossom. Sometimes frost will interrupt the display; usually not.

Another member of the ivy family that flowers in November is *Fatsia japonica*. This very large, bold evergreen shrub is made almost frivolous by its panicles of white flower umbels. Nearby is its hybrid with ivy, × *Fatshedera lizei*, whose main point is its lustrous foliage but that too is having a go at flowering.

Mahonias

Some of the flowering mahonias make their mark just now, putting on a colourful display in friendly yellows. Best for its foliage is *Mahonia oiwakensis* subsp. *lomariifolia* – a long leaf with numerous incurving leaflets. None of its hybrids can match it in this respect. The clustered flower strands are upright and so is the shrub's habit. Beside it is *M. japonica*, which is a not very striking shrub but has lemon-yellow flowers over a

long season, only just starting, and with a powerful lily-of-the-valley fragrance.

The crosses between these two are classified as *M. × media*. They are all showier than their parents, but have little or none of the lily-of-the-valley scent. 'Lionel Fortescue' has upright flower bunches, which look great if you can see them against a blue sky, while the flower strands of 'Buckland' (see below) are borne more horizontally.

Ice in November to carry a duck,
Rest of the winter all sludder and muck.

English proverb

Bulbs

Immense numbers of bulbs need to be planted – the majority, tulips. We sorted our own tulips over during the summer, separating those that looked large enough to flower next spring from those that didn't. The latter get rowed out to grow on, but often have to wait till December.

We shall have ordered and received a whole lot more tulips, the larger quantities for our bedding projects. First the carpeters are planted; then the tulips are all set out in their positions for planting (the bulbs having first been rolled in a fungicidal powder to protect them from botrytis). We also think of places where we can plant tulips among perennials. And then there are the ones that will be grown for display in large containers.

There are narcissi, hyacinths and crocuses, too. The narcissi should really be planted first, ideally in September, as they become active early, but they still have to

Tulips (here *Tulipa linifolia* Batalinii Group 'Bright Gem' flowering at Dixter in spring) are forgiving; you can keep them waiting before planting. As long as they've been in a cool place and haven't sprouted unduly, no harm results.

wait. Shoots on the paperwhites, *Narcissus papyraceus*, are often quite long before we get around to them, but the problem with them is to hold them back till Christmas or later, not how to bring them on. Once they are potted, I keep them as cool as I dare, short of allowing them to be frosted.

Most of these bulbs, in their display pots, go into a cold frame and all we need to do is to cover them with glass, if the weather is wet or frosty, but to remember not to leave them covered for so long that they dry out. Although not forced, this slight protection tends to bring them into flower noticeably earlier than those planted outside.

Some bulbs we'll use for naturalizing. I am careful to plant in a random fashion, with different intervals between each hole made. Otherwise you find that the bulbs are in straight lines. Neither do you want to plant them in circles.

Planting tulips

Using a narrow trowel, we plant only 5–7cm/2–3in or so deep. We just lever the soil to one side, pop the bulb in and there you are, one every five seconds or so, which allows for moving your own position.

Ferns and grasses

Of almost spring-like freshness is the foliage, produced quite late in the growing season, of the polypody fern, *Polypodium interjectum* 'Cornubiense' (see below), and that is seen beside the very newest leaves of another long-season performer, *Arum italicum* 'Pictum'.

Yet we can expect our first hoar frost, too, and that makes the aster hedges look as though they are flowering a second time.

November is a month of all seasons and a reminder that the year is a cycle, without beginning or end.

Flowering grasses are very good now, although the cultivars of *Molinia caerulea* suddenly disintegrate. One of the best is the late but regularly flowering *Panicum virgatum* 'Rubrum' (1.2m/4ft), with open-textured panicles and a reddish tinge. That lasts a long while.

Other jobs for the month

Sowing

O Sow all the spring bedding and early summer bedding such as lupins, aquilegias, verbascums, foxgloves, sweet rocket, anchusas, sweet Williams and perennial dianthus grown as biennials.

Routine care

O Give frost protection to all tender plants.
O Wrap plants that will not be housed, notably bananas, *Musa basjoo*, in a thick overcoat of male fern fronds that have been cut before they withered. Top up the wrapping after a few weeks, so that the banana's snout continues to be protected.
O Dig up and place cannas and dahlias in boxes of old potting soil, so that their tubers or rhizomes are the better able to remain plump. Store in a cellar or other frost-free area. Now and again, through the winter, give them a watering.
O Transplant carpeters such as double daisies, doronicums and various types of wallflowers, as well as the self-sown forget-me-nots, if appropriate.
O Give lawns and other grassy areas a final cut for the season.
O Start the winter digging as soon as a plot has been vacated. Before digging, dress the ground liberally with compost. Leave rough, over-large clods for the frost to break down.

Gardening in November

I have to admit that the weather, as well as the day length, can be most uncooperative, but Fergus has a system of laying out boards to stand on when planting, so that the planter's weight is distributed and does not hopelessly poach the ground where he has stood. The ideal is to clear away the summer bedding and replant all in one swoop, if not in one day. You will find that the ground under the old bedding is always friable and reasonably dry, until this cover is removed. If you can immediately fork it over and plant, conditions will be ideal. But woe betide if you fork over and have no daylight left to do the planting. Sure as fate, it will rain overnight and all those air spaces that have been created will fill with water like a sponge. If it was a frost that threatened, you could at least cover the ground, overnight, with hessian or tarpaulin, so as not to have to wait for a thaw the next morning before planting can be resumed.

December

December could be as dreary a month as
January, but the festive season prevents
this and provides a much-needed break.
Even the weeds understand the rules;
their growth has almost come to a standstill.
But the forward pulse of the year is evident
from week to week, if not from day to day.
The much-loved garden, all that's new in
it and all that's old, is barely marking time
and we are ready to steer it forward into
another year.

The best of Dixter in December

Winter flowerers

Wands of winter jasmine buds, *Jasminum nudiflorum*, are at their readiest to open, this month; such a cheerful shade of yellow.

Meanwhile *Cotoneaster horizontalis* continues its dazzling display for the first ten days, while *Spiraea thunbergii* puts on a final act. The female *Skimmia japonica* has clusters of large crimson berries which will last through the winter untouched by birds. But, as its growth is now slow, the berries show up all the better, not being much concealed by the young shoots of the previous season.

Chinese witch hazel, *Hamamelis mollis*, has a delicious, spicy fragrance, best enjoyed indoors. It needs to be coaxed a little, but only a little, to have it in flower for Christmas. Picking it ten days beforehand will certainly do the trick. I would far rather have that than silver or gold glitter on teasel heads in the house at this festive time of year. Its flowers (unlike those of wintersweet, *Chimonanthus praecox*) are amazingly frost hardy, while its rounded, hazel-like leaves are liable to a marginal leaf scorch, in summer, but we correct this with wood ash applied to it from my winter fires. As a shrub, witch hazel is pretty boring in the summer and that goes for a number of others of these winter flowerers, so they are scattered around the garden, where they

I raid our two specimens of Chinese witch hazel, given us in the 1930s, for their flowering branches.

can be absorbed by their neighbours in the summer.

I also have a young plant (too young to pick from, alas) of *Hamamelis × intermedia* 'Pallida', which is a lighter, brighter shade of yellow and has longer petals. It is much the showiest of the witch hazels. I know the red-flowered kinds have their advocates, but it is a pretty muted sort of red with little garden impact and I don't really see the point, unless you're making a collection.

Prunus × subhirtella 'Autumnalis Rosea' has a long and broken season, greatly affected by weather. If the winter is prolonged and cold, it may not be at its best till March, but in most years it reaches its peak in mid-December. That, of course, is a must for picking. My specimen, dating back to 1940 or thereabouts, has only just been dismissed and I made sure, before that happened, that I had a strong youngster, struck from a cutting off the old tree, with which to replace it. The original was a standard, which is normal, but makes it unnecessarily difficult to plunder for branches to bring indoors. Most of them are within the reach only of a long-arm pruner. The replacement will be a bush and therefore far more accessible. It may make a multi-stemmed tree in course of time. I don't want every tree to be on a leg.

My *Skimmia japonica* is self-sown and cramped between paving stones. It is also in full sun, which doesn't really suit its best health, so its foliage is yellowish.

Wintersweet

Branches of wintersweet, *Chimonanthus praecox* (see below) are especially welcome for bringing indoors, though their spicy fragrance is soon lost if kept in a warm room.

Our oldest wintersweet must date back to 1920, or thereabouts. It was given to my mother by our neighbours. Not knowing its ways, she thought it a dead loss as it did not flower for the first six years or so. This is normal, in seedlings, but once they do start they never fail. However, they do need plenty of sun heat to ripen their wood and coax them into setting flower buds. We have several plants, now, one of them a brighter, cleaner shade of yellow than the others, which are dingily coloured, but the scent's the thing – a wonderful spicy aroma on the air. First blooms normally open late November, a peak being reached at the turn of the year.

I should like to record my hope that no one, for lack of personal creativity, will fall back on the old cliché of recreating this, that or the other with the same plants that Christopher Lloyd used and in the same way.

Frosted plants

Frosts become more frequent as the month progresses, but there are far longer periods when the horse pond (see opposite) is unfrozen and can reflect the plants around it, notably the dogwoods. Now that the old water lily pads are vanishing, we can enjoy a far larger surface area of water and the pond seems twice itself, especially as it is full to its overflow. This is a very large pipe, installed by my father, which takes excess water underground right across the garden and down to the lower moat, on our boundary.

Skeletons of ornamental grasses play a large role in the December garden, especially the various cultivars of *Miscanthus sinensis* (see below). Best and most persistent of the lot, however, are the clustered stair-rods of *Calamagrostis* × *acutiflora* 'Karl Foerster'. They are pale and luminous even in the darkest weather.

About the author and his garden

Christopher Lloyd 1921–2006

Having described my gardening year, month by month, in this journal I have a clear duty to explain who I am, where I live and why I should be writing about my garden at all. My own interest in gardening goes back as far as I can remember, and it was encouraged by both my parents. I studied horticulture, and then taught it, at Wye College in Kent, but in 1954 returned home, to Great Dixter, and started a nursery devoted to the kinds of plants, many of them unusual, which grew in the garden. An all-important change and improvement in the fortunes of Dixter came about in 1993, when Fergus Garrett became head gardener. Till then, many areas in our labour-intensive garden were semi-neglected. I could see what needed doing to them and did what I could myself, but there was insufficient dynamism – or staff – to do the job thoroughly. Since then, we have had the whale of a time, and most visitors have loved the changes we made to the garden (some, of course, disapproved, and some thought I was mad). It has been a wonderful opportunity for experimenting.

The number of paying visitors increased with the years, which helped financially but imposed its own pressures. Like others in our position, we wished visitors spread themselves more evenly over the open season. We could only marginally bring that about by ensuring that the gardens were worth visiting in spring and autumn, as much as in the popular summer period. But that was a challenge that we enjoyed meeting and we loved the demands and rewards of a high-maintenance garden, which this certainly was. We are plantsmen, loving plants for their own sake as well as thinking out effective ways to use them.

My great good fortune has been in having been able to make my home into a going business concern. In fact, I have written about Great Dixter for many years, since it was my main quarry for innumerable gardening articles, started in 1952. I wrote in every issue of the weekly magazine *Country Life* since 1963, did a weekly piece for the *Guardian*, and also contributed frequently to America's *Horticulture* magazine and to the Royal Horticultural Society's journal, *The Garden*. I don't know how many books I have clocked up – quite a large number, of which I consider *The Well-Tempered Garden* to be seminal.

The garden

Dixter, a manor house, is a large timber-framed building constructed around 1460 and situated in the high weald. The weald of Kent and Sussex lies between the chalk of the North and South Downs, in south-east England, and the high weald is the centre

Lutyens designed the garden walls at Great Dixter and
how the hedges should run, which is not in the least
stodgy or predictable.

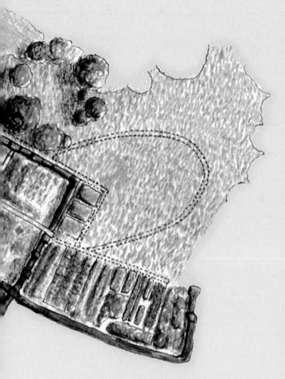

has been considerably mitigated. The gardens lie around the house, which is roughly in their centre, so that you have only to walk around the building to have made the garden circuit. It is a satisfyingly intimate arrangement.

There is a topiary and a sunk garden, which has an octagonal pool (two opposite sides are longer than the other six, which makes it look relaxed) surrounded by flagstone paving; then dry walling up to grass slopes, and so to the garden's main level, the framework being barns on two sides, a Lutyens wall on the third and a yew hedge on the fourth. The gardens throughout consist of mixed borders where annuals and bedding plants are worked in (rather than given beds to themselves) among shrubs and perennials. There are two small meadow areas, one of which goes right up to the south-east end of the house. Planted with lilacs, it is notable chiefly for its display of goldilocks, *Ranunculus auricomus* – which is a small, early-flowering buttercup – lady's smock and wood anemones. No one wittingly introduced them but they could hardly be improved upon. We call this the cats' garden, because in the old days the kitchen cats had their stronghold in the boiler house, here.

Christopher Lloyd

part of this area. Dixter is sited on a south-west-facing slope 55m/180ft above sea level (the sea being some 16 kilometres/10 miles distant), and although not very high it is near the top of its hill and commands all-round views (once you have stepped outside the garden) in every direction except east. Wind is a great enemy to gardening, and we have blithely planted out our views with trees and hedges so that wind damage

Index of plants